MORE MEMORIES
OF
York

The publishers would like to thank the following companies for their support in the production of this book

William Anelay Ltd

Askham Bryan College

William Birch & Sons Ltd

Hogg Builders (York) Ltd

Ingleby's Coaches

Monk Bridge Construction

Pilcher Homes Limited

J H Shouksmith & Sons Limited

Turnbulls York Ltd

Wrights of Crockey Hill

First published in Great Britain by True North Books Limited
England HX3 6AE
01422 344344

ISBN 1 903204 94 1

Text, design and origination by True North Books
Printed and bound by The Amadeus Press

MORE MEMORIES
OF
York

CONTENTS

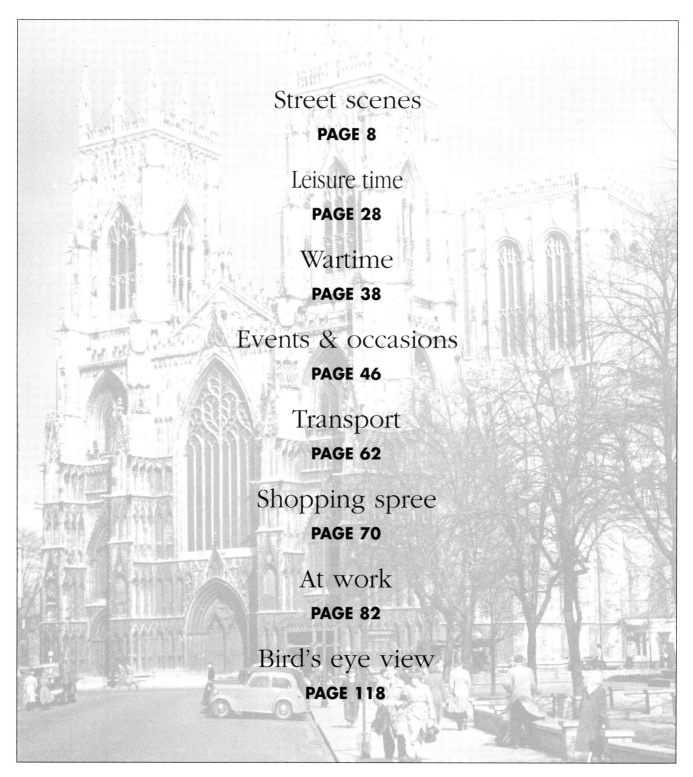

Street scenes
PAGE 8

Leisure time
PAGE 28

Wartime
PAGE 38

Events & occasions
PAGE 46

Transport
PAGE 62

Shopping spree
PAGE 70

At work
PAGE 82

Bird's eye view
PAGE 118

INTRODUCTION

Welcome to a book that will bring readers nostalgic photographs and written commentaries on events, places and people from the last century, with particular emphasis on the era that was current in our parents' and grandparents' lives. 'More Memories of York' is not a dry and dusty history book, but a thoughtful and carefully put together stroll down memory lane, taking in the sights that, in many cases, have changed beyond recognition, However, amidst this evidence of flux, there is also a reassuring element of the traditional that is still with us. Pedestrianisation and burger bars may have arrived, but the Minster, the Shambles, Ye Old Starre Inn and many more historic places remain, their souls barely touched by the cult of change for change's sake.

True North publications take a great pride in reminding readers of how things used to look and how the pace of life was set in the time of previous generations. It makes no apologies for taking a backward glance and allowing you to wallow a little in the glow of nostalgia. However, at the same time, the images and captions do not take a completely rosy view of the years that went before and acknowledge that deprivation and destruction also played their part in making us what we are

and our city what it is today. To look at the past gives us a better understanding of where we are now and where we might be in the future as this century unfolds. A life of beer and skittles has become one of alcopops and online gaming, but where will it be 50 years from now? At that we can only guess, but we can, perhaps, make an informed guess from the pattern that emerges as we trace the events along the timeline of the first three quarters of the 20th century that is reflected within these pages.

Of course, our city has a long and illustrious heritage that goes back two millennia. Founded in AD 71, York was the capital of the Roman province of Britannia Inferior. First known by the Latin name of Eboracum that was possibly inspired by a similar title given to a city in what is now Portugal, York was thus established as 'the place of the yew trees'. The Roman 9th Legion established a fort on the banks of the Ouse that would eventually enclose some 50 acres and house a garrison that was 6,000 strong. As with all military settlements, a small town grew around the fort, acting as a form of service industry to the personnel within. The headquarters of the legions was situated approximately on the site of the Minster and some evidence of the original city walls that the Romans built are still

with us. However, the walls were largely rebuilt by the Danes in the 9th century, with further restoration work taking place in medieval times. York was so important to the Romans that they built a royal palace here and the town eventually became the capital of northern Britannia.

By the early 5th century, the decline of the Roman Empire saw the legions leave Britain and it fell to the Saxons to assume a position of power. Eboracum was rechristened Eoferwic and established as the capital of the kingdom of Deirwa. During the 7th century much of pagan Britain converted to Christianity. A wooden church, the forerunner of the Minster, was erected, though this soon gave way to a stone one that was dedicated to St Peter. A more impressive edifice replaced this in the 8th century after a fire destroyed the church and accompanying school and library. However, it would not be until 1472 that a cathedral would finally be completed as a consecrated building. The intervening years had seen much in the way of rebuilding, fire damage, more remodelling and changes in style and emphasis. Sad to say, the cathedral did not have long to live in its full glory as the ravages of the Reformation took their toll during the 16th century. It would be another two or three centuries before more restoration elevated the mighty Minster to its true glory again.

York had become a farming community under the Vikings as these warlike 9th century invaders turned to more peaceful ways after taking the town and renaming it Jorvik. Under them, it became a major river port, part of extensive trading routes throughout northern Europe. The city walls were extended and new streets laid out. However, it was time for a change of influence yet again. Eric Bloodaxe, the last Viking to rule Jorvik, was driven out in 954, but it was only just over a century later that the Normans gained ascendancy. York's influence grew as the town prospered over several centuries, but there were hard times to come. The important wool industry relocated and, as a religious centre, the town suffered badly at the hands of successive Tudor monarchs and their policies.

Revival came during the Jacobean and Georgian phases that saw York become a genteel and socially desirable place to be. Her role and reputation as the social and cultural centre for wealthy northerners was on the up and up. London's lead was followed as new coffeehouses appeared and became popular social centres. One of the most common activities at coffeehouses was discussing local news and events that were outlined in York's first newspaper, 'The York Mercury', published from 1719. This ambience of gentility was to be replaced by the steam and smoke of the industrial revolution as one of its major offshoots

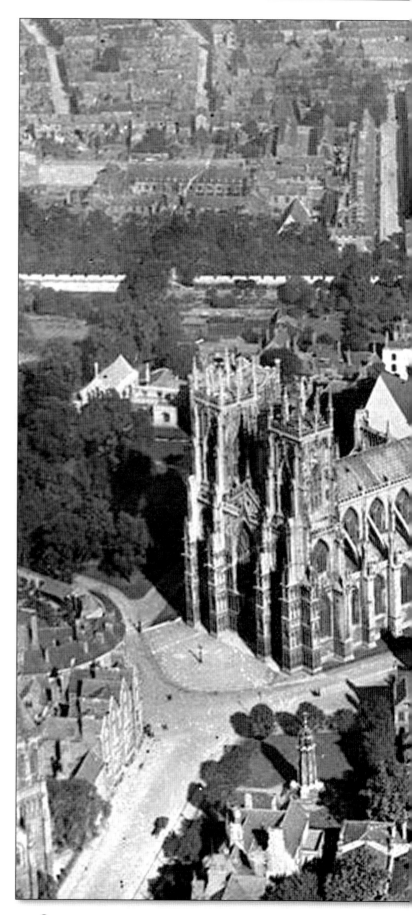

An aerial view of York Minster circa 1920

made its mark here in the Victorian era. The railway age arrived here in 1839. York was well placed to become the epicentre of the earth shattering impact that the days of steam locomotion would bring to Britain. Situated midway between Edinburgh and London, it was not surprising that industries involving carriage manufacture and repair, as well as other associated businesses, soon flourished. The population swelled as workers and their families moved in. The railway provided other industries an opportunity to move goods quickly and soon other business ventures, such as Rowntree's, found this a convenient base from where to operate. York became a city in 1887, at last acknowledging its historical, cultural and now industrial standing.

Now we turn to the last century with the pages that make up the literary and photographic time capsule that is 'More Memories of York'. Younger readers will enjoy seeing for themselves the Muriel Lyon ladies outfitter business on Micklegate Hill where granny purchased her 'New Look' dress after the war. They will smile at the Morris Cowley and Riley Elf that were once their uncles' pride and joy being driven along Parliament Street and comment on the Charleston and Black Bottom being performed at the exotically named Danse Salon on Blossom Street, above the Crescent Café. As we look back over the years we will all see how buildings, social mores, language and lifestyles have all undergone alterations. As the first pages are turned, this book will help readers relive the days when trams ran along Market Street, men stood up on buses to offer ladies their seats, shopkeepers sold cloth by the yard and not the metre and 'keep off the grass' was an instruction in a park and not one given to a university student. It is time to get into that wistful mood of thinking of occasions past when grandpa celebrated City's elevation to the Football League, dad was going off to pilot a Hurricane in the Battle of Britain or we were reading about Dan Dare in the Eagle. Why not suck on a Spangle or have a sip of dandelion and burdock from a stoppered bottle? Put Neil Sedaka's 'Oh Carol' onto the Dansette record player and let the waves of nostalgia start to flow.

York has much to be proud of, and a number of its best known and longest established firms have allowed us to access their internal archives. This has enabled us to recount the history of these companies from humble beginnings, in most cases, to leading positions in their chosen area of expertise. These organisations have tremendous social, as well as commercial significance, as between them they represent the places of employment for many thousands of York people. We are very grateful to the directors of these businesses for their co-operation and valuable support. Let the nostalgia begin.

STREET SCENES

Low Petergate is now part of the pedestrianised centre of the city. In 1900, though, there was no need to have restrictions on the movement of motor cars as the good old horse was the power that moved the carts, wagons and private cabs along the road. Looking towards the Minster, we can see a brewer's dray loaded with barrels of the amber nectar served at such hostelries as the Fox Inn, Garrick's Head and Londesboro Arms. This latter inn was the final public house to close on this street. A plaque on its wall commemorating the coming of the railway to York was unveiled in 1978. However, it ceased trading in 1987 and was turned into a pizza parlour. The roadway in this old photograph was covered in horse droppings and, although these might be of some use to a gardener, they made walking off the pavement a messy and smelly business. The infamous Guy Fawkes was born near here in 1570. He was educated at St Peter's School, Clifton. No doubt he took a special interest in chemistry lessons to acquire a knowledge of explosives that he would attempt to put to use in 1605. Low Petergate had a variety of shops at the start of the 20th century that included an outlet selling rope, a printer, a library and a brush maker.

Below: This is 'the street of butchers', as the Shambles has also been known. Records show that there were 26 butchers here in mid Victorian times. The name of the street comes from an old word that meant bench or booth. Animals were slaughtered on the Shambles and the meat was served over what are now the shop window bottoms or 'shamels'. The raised pavements provided a channel down which butchers could wash away the animals' blood. It is York's oldest street and was even mentioned in the Domesday Book. It was rebuilt in c1400, when it assumed its present character. The roofs project out above the narrow street and almost touch their opposite neighbours in some places. There is a shrine halfway along the street dedicated to the memory of a former resident. Margaret Clitherow's house was used as a safe haven for Catholic priests during Elizabethan times, a dangerous practice she maintained for 12 years. She was sentenced to death for her activities and was pressed by being crushed by a heavy weight on Ouse Bridge in 1586. She was canonised in 1970. The boys dominating the foreground of this 1900 photograph were passing displays of meat laid out on the shamels. Behind them, girls dressed in ankle length dresses can be seen, with a horse and cart further in the distance. The Eagle and Child public house is to the right.

Above: Stonegate was pedestrianised in the early 1970s but, apart from that, the scene along here has changed little in the intervening years since this photograph was taken around the time of World War I. Just as it was in the 1910s, Stonegate is still the main shopping street in the Minster region of the city. The old buildings, despite conversions to gift shops, coffee houses etc, have retained much of their period feel. Modern buskers entertain shoppers now, but you can still imagine the jugglers and street artists who performed here in earlier times. The beam pub sign to the Old Starre Inn continues to dominate the view along here. It was first erected in 1793, though the inn itself has a much longer history. Documents trace its history back to 1644 and one landlord is recorded as being miffed at having to serve ale to Roundheads during the Civil War as he was a Royalist. The pub's cellar is said to have been used as an operating theatre after the Battle of Marston Moor. Many of York's historic buildings have ghost stories linked with them and the Old Starre is no exception. One tells of two cats being bricked up in a pillar and that they can sometimes be heard scampering through the inn. Dogs are said to bark at the pillar and try to reach the moggies, while others suggest that it is their owners who are barking if they believe the story.

Below: It must have been a very strange sort of person who indulged in all these forbidden activities and, to boot, at the same time. The thought of someone playing cricket and soccer while shaking out his carpet creates a quite surreal picture. But, the powers that be just love to put up signs that forbid both the innocent and the socially unacceptable alike. We have even come across notices that state 'keep off the grass' in a public park. Elsewhere, you can find, pasted in a hotel bathroom above a hot water tap, 'take care, this water is hot'. We can forgive someone writing below, 'so it should be'. The photograph dates from the 1910s and shows a sign attached to the Herdsman's Cottage on Heslington Road, at the edge of Walmgate Stray. Perhaps some youth of the day got an early 20th century form of ASBO for waving his Wilton about. All together, there are four Strays of open ground within the city: Monk, Walmgate, Micklegate and Bootham. They are a relic of the days when even greater tracts of common land were available to the Freemen as grazing for their cattle. Following the Enclosures Acts of the 18th and 19th century, many of these rights were restricted. Each Stray was overseen by a Pasture Manager, but in 1905 the city took over the administration of Micklegate Stray. The other three followed suit after World War II.

We do like to fly the flag whenever we can and there was quite a bit of it around the turn into the 20th century. In 1897, there were great celebrations as Queen Victoria reached her diamond jubilee after 60 years on the throne. The nation took to the streets again in 1902 and 1911 to honour the coronations of Victoria's son and grandson. However, this photograph does not depict any such national event. This festivity was restricted to the people of York. Here, residents on Hungate put out their flags and strung up their bunting to mark the centenary of the 13 men's and 12 women's adult schools that took place on Sunday, 13 October 1907. Some 2,000 flocked to the Theatre Royal to take tea and watch a slide show of Adult School events and listen to a succession of speakers. The style of dress favoured by those on view is typically Edwardian. Although the elderly woman on the right strikes a Victorian pose and is probably a widow, as evidenced by her black clothing, the younger folk are much more in vogue. The bustle and heavy petticoats have gone, along with the face hiding poke bonnet. More lightweight dresses, cut to fit snugly at the hips, give a more feminine style than that of previous century. For men and boys, though, the suit and flat cap still had plenty of life in them just yet.

Below: Every visiting monarch and head of state has passed through this stone gateway, which has stood guard over the city for 800 years. Micklegate Bar, a corruption of Mickleith, meaning 'great gate', was formerly a wooden structure dating from Norman times. It was the most frequently used entrance to the city and was thus the obvious place to display the severed heads of a variety of traitors, rebels and conspirators as a warning to those planning a little bit of subversion. .The tram was moving from Queen Street into Blossom Street in the early 1910s. Nunnery Lane is off to the right. Blossom Street was part of the main London road until 1772. The Punch Bowl Inn on the right hand corner is still flourishing today as part of the Wetherspoon chain. When this image was captured the landlord was Robert Thompson. The inn was named after one of the symbols associated with the Whig party, but is thought to have been the site of a house of ill repute during Tudor times and that a young woman met her untimely end at the hands of drunken patron. The ghost of this lady roams the building in an eternal attempt to escape from the clutches of her murderer. The sign above the tram advertised Warriner's cycle works and garage on Toft Green. The shop on the left now belongs to a driving school.

Above: What an Aladdin's cave of goodies was laid out to tempt the sweet teeth of these children gazing in through the shop window on North Street one day in the 1920s. They looked longingly at jars of boiled sweets, wine gums, bullseyes and gobstoppers. This street has its origins in the 12th century and became a hotch potch of warehouses, yards and alleys that led down to the river. Much of the area was redeveloped in the 1960s to include a hotel, garden and waterside walk. The establishment was a typical corner shop, selling a variety of groceries, cigarettes and confectionery. It was owned by the Hemmens family and, at this time, was run by Arthur. He was born in London in 1850, but moved here as a baby to the shop that his aunt owned. He took over the business and ran it until he was well beyond retirement age. He died in 1944. His daughter, Christiana, known to everyone as Cissie, carried on the family business into her advancing years until she called it a day in 1968 after a robbery left her traumatised. She was 98 when she died in 1984. The Park Drive cigarettes being advertised belonged to one of the cheaper brands manufactured by Gallaher's that rivalled the popular Wills' Woodbine. The cards of footballers, cricketers, flowers, famous places etc that the packets contained have since become very collectable.

Above: Nos 5 and 6 Hill's Yard are shown as they appeared in c1933. The yard opened out off Navigation Road and into Walmgate, where two people can be seen in the distance. The yard was also known as Marston's Yard. The mangle seen by the dustbins was one of the essential pieces of equipment in any household during the interwar years. This mechanical laundry aid consisted of two rollers in a sturdy frame, connected by cogs and powered by a hand crank that meant that housewives developed strong biceps in their right arms as they laboured away getting the bulk of the water out of the washing. The machine was invented in the 18th century as a cheaper alternative to the box mangle used by the middle classes and commercial laundries. The mangle went hand in glove with the dolly tub where the week's dirty clothing was washed, with a little help by being stirred and prodded by a pole known as a posser. Many of those who lived in this part of the city were descended from Irish immigrants who fled here in the 1840s after successive years of potato famine. Their only future was poverty and starvation, so they left their homeland and fled overseas. Many emigrated to America, while others contented themselves with a life closer to their roots.

Below: Two horse drawn buses were delivered in October 1880 to link the centre with Castle Mills Bridge, the terminus of the horse tramway. A pair of steam cars was used around this time, but they did not last long in service as the public complained about the noise and dirt. Obviously, they did not object to the horses as locals were keen rose and rhubarb growers. The first of the horse tramcars was a double decker built by Starbuck and Company. This was nothing to do with a coffee house, but a firm based in Birkenhead. By 1891, 37 horses were employed, sharing the load in pulling 10 tramcars. By the time of this c1920 photograph, electrification of the tramway had long been completed. The car leading the way was passing over Queen Street Bridge. The imposing building is that of the Station Hotel. It opened in 1878, a year after the railway station. The hotel's grand size helped hide some of the uglier nature of the railway lines and workings. It also suggested the solidarity, reliability and influence of rail transport. Even so, it was not considered large enough as demand increased in the late 19th century and the hotel was extended in 1894. The track to the original station can be made out at the bottom right of the picture.

Above: Lower Wesley Place, Hungate was swamped by the floodwater that rose at an alarming rate on 28th February 1933. In 1931, the city was hit by the worst flooding it had seen in 40 years, only to be under water again the following year. It tested resilience to the limit when residents had to start mopping up for the third time in less than three years. Standing on a raised walkway, the woman with the sweeping brush could only make a token attempt at resistance as her front doorstep was breached yet again. Children at the far end of the street splashed around in the filthy water, oblivious to the dangers of what germs and bacteria lay within those murky depths. A local reporter described how he had swum from the Guildhall to the Museum Gardens. Whether he was taking the risk of contracting some nasty disease in the interests of first hand journalism is not known, but he chanced his arm as he could well have been an obituary item in the not too distant future. Perhaps he should have devoted his column inches to describing how the poorer areas of the city were amongst the worst affected. The poverty trap was not just about money but housing conditions as well. The poor could not afford to move to safer homes and it was those who were the most vulnerable who suffered over and over again.

Below: They seemed happy with their lot as they stood on a raised walkway in Wray's Yard, Hungate on 28th February 1933. Still, if you live in York you have become

accustomed to the floodwater that seems to be a regular occurrence. Over the years there have been mopping up operations galore and countless plans to improve defences, but still Mother Nature wins hands down. Some areas are just more prone to flooding than others, but York does seem to be one of the worst affected places in the country. There was a lot of money spent on improving the city's capability to withstand the after effects of heavy and prolonged rainfall following the 1982 floods, but half a century earlier all this group pictured here could do was to grin and bear it. Although the incursion of water into homes and businesses damages property and possessions, it is the aftermath that is even worse. The cleaning up operation is as prolonged as the stench that accompanies each disaster. Sadly, York became so used to it happening that locals often just single out the worst ones, such as 1947, 1982 and 2000.

Below: Dating from the 1930s, this view of York Minster was taken from Duncombe Place. It shows the building in all its magnificence. The Minster is the largest Gothic cathedral in northern Europe and is the seat of the second most important office in the Church of England. Various places of worship had stood on the site over some five or six centuries, until Walter de Gray became Archbishop of York in 1215, inheriting a site with buildings that seemed to lack a sense or order or purpose. He commissioned the building of an appropriate cathedral and work began in 1220. The first structures were completed in the 1250s, but it would be a further two centuries before it was finally consecrated. However, the Minster did not fare well during the following century. It suffered at the hands of the Reformationists and was stripped of many of its treasures. It recovered, but several fires during Victorian times left it in need of further renovation. The Minster's fortunes revived in the 20th century as concentrated efforts were made to restore it to its true glory. It became one of the major tourist attractions in the north of England. In July 1984, a fierce fire took hold, concentrated in the 13th century south transept and left its roof destroyed. It took four years to complete repairs at a cost of £2.25million, but the Minster was finally re-dedicated in a service attended by the Queen in November 1988.

Above: This was clearly a wartime scene on Blossom Street. The black and white markings on the bollards and the flashes on the kerbstones were part of the measures taken to help motorists and pedestrians during the blackout that was imposed as part of our attempt to hinder the enemy as it attacked our towns and cities from the air. However, the restrictions caused problems on the ground. Introduced right at the start of the war, regulations meant that initially cars were only allowed to use sidelights. These were tiny pinpricks in the night. The results were alarming. Car accidents increased and the number of people killed on the roads almost doubled. The government changed its stance and dipped headlights were permitted, as long as the driver had headlamp covers with three horizontal slits. A 20 mph speed limit was imposed on night drivers. Ironically, the first man to be convicted for this offence was driving a hearse. In the photograph an old style Belisha crossing can be seen. Named for the former Minister of Transport, Leslie Hore-Belisha, it had studs on the road to mark the crossing. The black and white markings of the zebra did not appear until 1951.

The car on the left was parked on Bootham outside the Exhibition Hotel, with Lupton's chemist shop just beyond. The name of the road and surrounding district is said to have been derived from an ancient description as 'the place of the booths', referring to the poor huts located just outside the city walls. The Exhibition is just opposite Bootham Bar, one of York's old gateways into the historic city. Bootham Bar marks the northern entrance to the city, on the Great North Road. It is the only gate that still stands on the site of a previous Roman one and parts of its structure date from the 12th century. Bootham was originally a squalid street separated from the city by Bootham Bar and shut off from the graceful St Mary's Abbey by the Abbey walls. Access to the latter was only gained in the early 1900s when properties at the end of the roads were demolished. The district has large numbers of Georgian houses where pattern books were much used by local builders. Brick became the favoured building material over timber during these times. The bicycles parked outside the cast iron frontage of John Cross' family grocers demonstrate the trusting nature that our predecessors had. Other businesses here included the Plumes Hotel. Hilda Pearson's women's clothing shop, the Kilvington dairy and café and the Midland Bank.

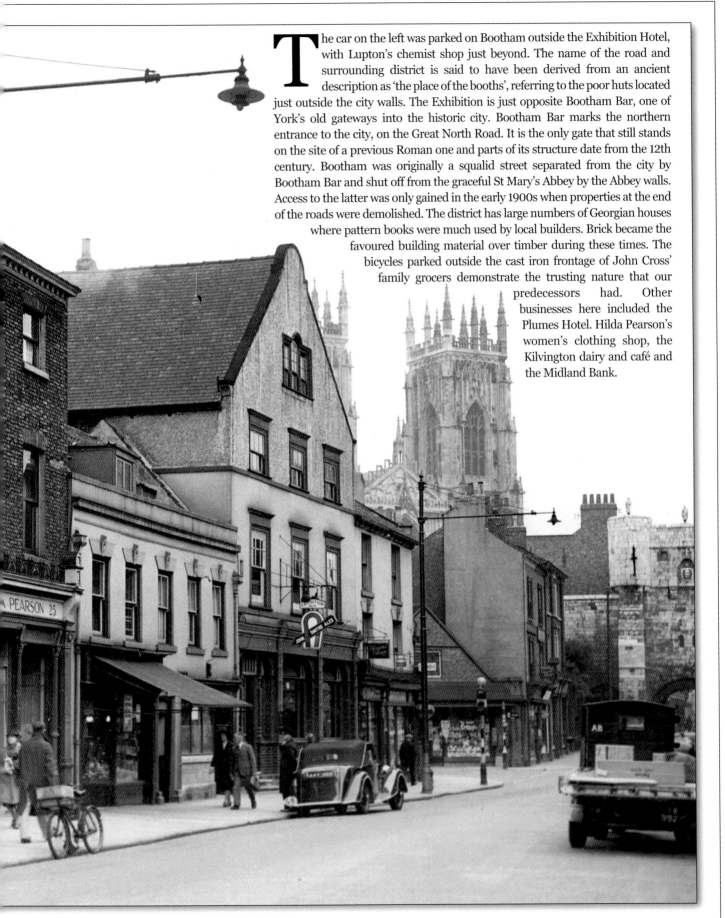

Below: The Bay Horse Inn is on Blossom Street, on the corner with Shaw's Terrace. Seen in c1940, the car outside the popular watering hole is a 9.8 horsepower Hillman. This was one of the models manufactured by the company founded by William Hillman in 1907. Based in Coventry, the firm was taken over by Rootes in 1928, but still manufactured cars under its traditional name. The Minx was, perhaps, the most famous of the Hillman range. The first appeared in 1932 and continued in production until 1970. The model in the photograph belonged to Dr RP McGarrigle of 92 The Mount. In the early 1940s, petrol was heavily rationed to a degree that private motoring was heavily restricted in order that fuel stocks could be conserved and directed towards vehicles engaged in duties connected with the war effort. However, some people received preferential treatment and could get petrol over and above the normal ration if their need was considered essential. A doctor making house calls or needing to rush to those injured in air raids was classed as one who could obtain extra supplies and nobody begrudged him that.

Right: With Barker Lane and the YWCA to the right, Micklegate was photographed in this summery wartime scene in the early 1940s. A pile of sandbags on the pavement was part of the attempt to minimise the effect of the bombing raids that residents and businesses had become used to during those dark days. The YWCA hostel is a fine example of Georgian architecture that helps make this part of the city of interest to the visitor. Formerly Bathurst House, it was originally a two storey building before a further floor was added in the 1820s. It was known as the Central Hotel either side of World War I, before being taken over by the YWCA in 1921. This organisation for young Christian women was founded in 1855. The first hostel was opened on Upper Charlotte Street, London as a stopover point for Florence Nightingale's nurses en route to the Crimea. Micklegate House, the next one along in this picture, is also a fine Georgian edifice. Built in 1752, several decades later than its neighbour, it was designed by John Carr for John Bouchier of Beningbrough Hall. Although some of its original internal features have been stripped out, it still has its old staircase and some fireplaces. In its heyday, it was the finest house southwest of the river.

Below: York County Savings Bank dominates this image of the corner of Blake Street that is seen from Davygate. The car approaching the camera was an unusual sight on British roads. We were used to seeing Fords, Austins and Morrises, but this one came from Italy. Common enough now, but a Fiat, in this case a 6.7 horsepower model, was something of a rarity in 1940. Its headlights were shrouded because of blackout restrictions and further wartime evidence can be

gleaned from the letter 'S' on the far right that indicates the position of an air raid shelter. Blackout restrictions were brought in during the early days of the war to make life difficult for enemy aircraft to get a clear view of a potential target. At first, no light whatsoever was allowed on the streets. All street lights were turned off. Even the red glow from a cigarette was banned, and one man was convicted when he struck a match to look for his false teeth. It cost him a fine of 10s (50p). Later, permission was given for small torches to be used on the streets, providing the beam was masked by tissue paper and pointed downwards. To the left we can see the edge of Terry's Restaurant and, to the right of the bank, Hylda Anfield's millinery shop.

Left: The name of Scarrs, the hardware shop on the right hand side of Fossgate as we look towards Pavement in a view captured in 1940, was a poignant one for the chap walking towards the camera. He had a fair few scars of his own. Making his way on one leg, this unfortunate man had to struggle along with his wooden one. Maybe he was a casualty of the 1914-18 War that left so many of our brave boys crippled for life. Millions perished at the front, but there were so many others who were left without limbs, eyesight or healthy lungs and somehow had to rebuild their shattered lives. There were also those for whom the nightmares never went away and they suffered just as much as those whose injuries were plain to see. Now this man had to relive it all again as jackboots marched across Europe and the skies above Britain were filled with Heinkels and Junkers on their way to deliver their cargoes of destruction. The Electric Cinema, part of which can be seen on the right, was York's first purpose built picture house when it opened in 1911. Cinemagoers enjoyed a quiet pint after an evening at the movies in the Queen's Head across the road. This pub closed in 1956 and was demolished in 1964.

Above: Monday was the traditional washday for many. For working class families, the burden fell upon mum. Her role as a housewife meant that the day was spent boiling clothes in a tub and wringing them out through the mangle before pegging out on the line in the back yard. Reddened hands were her reward and she still had beds to make, carpets to beat and lino to wash. The kids needed feeding and she had to get hubby's evening meal ready. It was hard work and she had few, if any, modern electrical appliances or white goods to make the task of running the house any easier. Many families lived in terraced housing, some of it back to back, with outdoor lavvies where you learned to whistle with one foot against the door in case someone else attempted to enter this little enclave of privacy. Many yards still had a tin bath that was dragged inside and filled with kettles of boiling water before family members took it in turn to soak themselves. Dating from the 1950s, this was a typical scene of life in the George Street area of Walmgate. Families and communities were close knit, sharing each other's joys and sorrows. It was quite common to lend a neighbour a helping hand in times of need.

Below: Bootham Bar stands at the point originally occupied by the Roman entrance known as the Porta Principalis Dextra, although the outer archway dates from the Norman period. A door knocker was added in 1501 to be used by any Scotsman wishing to get permission to gain entry to the city. Due to its position near the western front of the Minster, it is probably the best known of York's city gates. It seems remarkable now that, once upon a time, the powers that be considered demolishing part of our city's heritage. In 1832, Bootham Bar was in a poor state and under threat. Only public pressure and its willingness to subscribe to its repair saved the day. The steps up to the walls were built in 1899. This image dates from 1955 during the era that saw us starting to turn the corner after the austerity of the immediate postwar years. Rationing had at long last ended the year before and the man in the street was beginning to feel more secure in his day to day life as work was almost guaranteed and the price of former luxury goods came within his reach. Ordinary families could afford televisions and washing machines, even if they were bought 'on tick'. The cost of a motor car such as the Ford Popular was something to be considered.

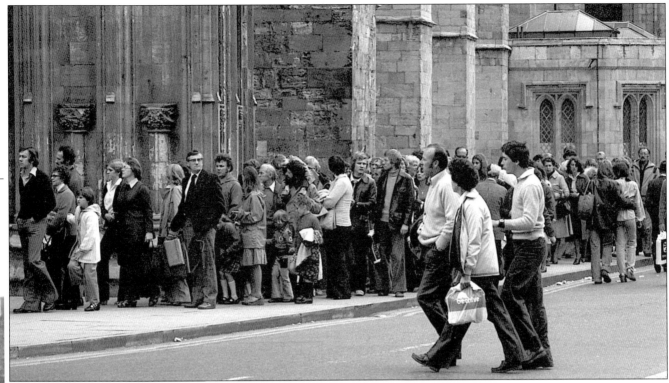

Above: York Minster is one of the country's top tourist attractions as well as being a major religious establishment, second only in importance in the Anglican Church to Canterbury Cathedral. It receives no financial support from central or local government for the building's upkeep and nowadays charges over £5 as an entry charge to maintain this holy and historic building. As this line of visitors queued for admission on a summer's day in 1978, the English Tourist Board conducted a census on behalf of the Cathedral Advisory Group, an organisation that included the Dean of York, Ronald Jasper (1917-90) among its members. He was a well respected historian and liturgist who retired from his post at the Minster in 1984. We hasten to add that his departure was not linked with the disastrous fire that devastated part of this historic building in the early hours of 9 July that year. Staff braved heavy smoke and flames to salvage the Minster's priceless artefacts while the building was still ablaze. The cause of the fire was unclear, but it is thought that it was struck by lightning.

LEISURE TIME

Entrants in the June 1978 Raft Race on the River Ouse are just passing under the Ouse bridge

Right: This is the interior of 37 Stonegate as it was furnished in 1906. The Edwardian parlour was not cluttered with a radio, television, DVD player and computer that took up space at different times of the 20th century. In fact, the electricity needed to power these pieces of equipment was a rarity in most homes a century ago. Gas lighting was the then modern form of illumination and home entertainment was provided by someone at the piano, by reading, indulging in embroidery or simply in conversing. When did we last spend a night in just chatting with friends and family? The long case clock, dresser for the best crockery and the writing desk or bureau were the must have items of furniture that

complemented the table, chairs and sofa. The buildings on Stonegate were a mixture of shops and private residences, with some of them combining both functions. Stepping outside No 37 would enable the owner to see M Wherley's watch and clockmaking shop, AE Pearson's cycle dealership, S Bell's piano business, RH Hawkswell's antiques emporium and the grandly named Eclectic Book Company. Stonegate was an ancient paved way that had its origins in Roman times as it heads towards the site of the former military headquarters. It got its modern name in medieval times when stone was moved from barges on the river near the Guildhall directly to the Minster.

Left: A cynic might point out, looking at the top of this photograph, that free insurance would be of little use to you if you did suffer a fatal accident. Whatever the interpretation of this slogan, we can be sure that we are looking at the Yorkshire Gazette tent at the Agricultural Show of July 1921. The Great Yorkshire Show, as most know it, was first held in 1838 and, since 1951, has had a purpose built home in Harrogate. This group of well dressed gentlemen, no T shirts and jeans in those days, included Alfred Humphries (1869-1952), head gardener at Backhouse Nursery in Acomb. His wife, Elsie, was the daughter of his predecessor in the job, so we expect that any children they had must have been born with the greenest of fingers, considering that pedigree. To the right of the group, a Ford wagon was for sale at £220, a not inconsiderable price in those days. The Knavesmire has been used for many activities over the years, including shows, air races and sheepdog trials. It has been a venue for racing since 1730 when flooding of the courses on Clifton and Clifford Ings prevented their use. In 1753 a subscription was opened to allow the building of a stand, completed the following year. It boasted offices and rooms for entertainment as well as a large meeting room with a veranda 200 feet in length.

Above: Mollie (Mary) Bagot Stack founded the League of Health and Beauty, now the Fitness League, in 1930, revolutionising exercise for women, leading the way forward and setting standards for an industry still in its infancy. She opened a class in central London and within three months it had over one thousand members. In order to get some publicity, Mollie organised a free display to the music of a military band by 150 members in Hyde Park. The demonstration was a huge success and afterwards press cuttings flooded in from all over the world. Her dream was to create a system of exercise structured and graded to the needs of all ages and abilities. Yet, she was not alone in her ideals. Rowntree's put on this display of physical training and dancing at its cocoa works on Haxby Road during the celebrations for Civic Week in June 1928. Companies opened their doors to the public and every one viewed it as a great success. Rowntree's had a reputation for a social conscience and demonstrated its willingness to support the growing interest in women's fitness. Cooped up all day on the factory floor, it was important that they got some fresh air and exercise. They might have shocked their mothers by displaying so much flesh, but the sense of freedom they enjoyed more than made up for any disapproving glances.

Right: These little boys were not on the edge of Sherwood Forest, but playing outside St Anthony's Hall on Aldwark. In this image from the 1940s they had probably been inspired by the swashbuckling Hollywood style of Errol Flynn as he rescued Olivia de Havilland as Maid Marian from the wicked clutches of his enemies in the popular movie that came to our cinemas just before the war. What would these little monkeys have made of today's politically correct regulations? Little boys were made to climb trees, let off bangers and get their legs muddy. No self respecting eight year old could face his peers unless he had grazes on his elbows and scabs on his knees. These lads did not complain that there was nothing for them to do. They did not expect to be spoon fed. They went out and made their own entertainment.

Left: What had this grand old dame seen during her long life? Elizabeth Johnson (1805-1907) was the oldest licensee in the country and ran the Bumper Castle on Wigginton Road for over 60 years. Quite a large pub, it is situated directly north of the city centre, just on the eastern edge of Clifton Moor. In Mrs Johnson's day, the Bumper would have got a lot of business from those employees of the nearby Rowntree's works who fancied a tipple. To put this old lady's life into perspective, in the year that she was born Nelson was winning and dying at Trafalgar, Thomas Jefferson began a second term of office as the American president and George III was still on the British throne. Elizabeth was turned 25 by the time that the first railway ran and would be in her 30s when a stripling of a girl called Victoria began her reign as our monarch. She would see the introduction of gas lighting on our streets and in our homes, the invention of the telephone, the first national postal service, the development of electricity, the great days of British shipyards and the first motor cars to appear on the road. Mrs Johnson was born at a time when much of England was a green and pleasant land, dominated by agriculture, but she left it as a place devoted to heavy industry and grime.

You could almost imagine the Cottingley fairies being placed at the bottom of this idyllic scene. It is quite a magical view of a little part of our green and pleasant land that could have inspired a great artist to paint it. Thankfully, we have the camera that was able to capture this view of swans on the lake in Acomb's West Park. Guiding her cygnet, mum was pictured on 29th March 1954. This was no ugly duckling, but a noble creature that would grow into an adult with a regal bearing. Swans are often a symbol of love or fidelity because of their long lasting monogamous relationship. As well as having the traditional bowling greens, rose garden, pergola walk, play equipment and open grass areas, this park has a delightful sylvan feel. There are mature woodlands and a former arboretum, with associated songbirds that can be heard trilling merrily among the branches. Considering that the park is within the boundaries of York's largest suburb, it takes on the role of an oasis of calm away from the hustle and bustle of 21st century life. The name 'Acomb' is derived from the old English for oak tree. Acomb Grange was once the residence of the masters of the great medieval hospital of St Leonard. Despite its built up state, the historic part of the village along Front Street and the Green retain their village character.

Below: The 1950s and the wonder and excitement of the acquisition of the first television set. Black and white of course and though this model was not one of the cheapest sets available then, the screen was probably only a modest twelve or fourteen inches. People then considered television a mere adjunct of radio and even the design of this set makes it look like a wireless. It may well have been acquired to enable the family (and others) to watch the Queen's Coronation in 1953. The dress of the young ladies admiring the set epitomises the 1950s, as does the small table lamp standing on its own 'mat' - so as not to damage this expensive and prized new piece of furniture.

Left: Hunter and Smallpage Ltd had an up-market furniture shop in Goodramgate, York. This advertisement from the mid-1950s shows a display of furniture available in their shop, being 'modelled' in a setting which featured playwright Michael Pertwee and his actress wife Valerie French. Note the small television receiver to the left of the couple. It looks almost comic now, but a set of these (small) dimensions would have been very advanced - and desirable at the time.

Below: A pleasant rowing trip was the order of the day for this lucky pair when this picture was taken in the early 1960s. York has always had so much to offer in terms of leisure and recreation and long-time residents are often a little guilty of taking it for granted. This photograph contains nothing in the way of grand monuments or well-known buildings, but it still manages to convey a delightful feeling of calm and relaxation which is characteristic of many areas in the city.

Below: It is still Bootham Crescent to most fans, despite the rebranding to KitKat Crescent that happened in 2005. York City purchased this stadium, a former cricket ground, in 1932. In March 1938, the ground's record attendance was reached as 28,123 people watched the match against Huddersfield Town. Those were heady days as the opponents were FA Cup finalists that year. The ground was badly damaged during the war when a bomb landed on the Shipton Street End. Floodlights were erected in 1959 and first used in a friendly against Newcastle United on 28 October. Ground improvements in the 1980s were made possible by the revenue from a good Cup run that included games against the might of Arsenal and Liverpool. Over the years, the ground capacity has fallen and only just over 9,000 can fit into Bootham Crescent these days. The club joined the Football League in 1929, but was relegated to the Conference in 2004. This photograph was taken on 25 November 1978 when City faced Blyth Spartans. The visitors had set the nation agog with interest earlier that year as they reached the fifth round of the FA Cup, an amazing feat for a non league side. We feared the worst when we were held to a 1-1 draw in the first round of the Cup, but managed to win the replay 5-3.

Above: Presumably there must have been some sort of handicapping system in force in this cycle relay race as the level of competition hardly looks as if it is on an even keel. Perhaps we are doing the youngsters on the right an injustice and that they were actually a July 1978 version of Chris Boardman and Jason Queally about to overtake the rider in front who does look a little puffed out, truth to tell. This was part of a T Club cycle rally taking place on Knavesmire. Situated in the southwest of the city, some distance outside the historic walls, Knavesmire's low-lying position makes it liable to severe flooding in times of heavy rain. As a consequence, it remained undeveloped as the city expanded around it. Much of its area is taken up by York Racecourse, but there is still plenty of room left for dog walkers and public events to take place. Included in the latter, in earlier times, were the public hangings that were carried out here. Dick Turpin, the notorious highwayman, was just one of those to have dangled here when he met his demise in 1739. The city elders decided that the sight of a scaffold did not give a good impression to those visiting York and executions were moved to a spot near to the castle. The last such event took place here in 1801 and a plaque now marks the place where the gallows once stood. On a happier note, Pope John Paul II celebrated marriage and family life in an address given here in May 1982 on one of his stops during his visit to Britain.

WARTIME

Below: This group of wardens from the Air Raid Precautions (ARP) branch of the Civil Defence, pictured during World War II, illustrates that women played an active role in the organisation. Churchill was later to refer to the fairer sex as 'the army that Hitler forgot'. They more than played their part, and not just in keeping the home fires burning. The Women's Voluntary Service (WVS), founded by Stella, Lady Reading, in 1938, recognised that war was coming and organised first aid and gas defence classes for civilians. When hostilities broke out, the WVS members could be found out and about during air raids, offering support and refreshment to others. In quieter moments they organized salvage drives and other fund raising activities. Other women joined the armed forces and played vital roles alongside their male colleagues by driving ambulances, planning air force operations and working on intelligence projects. Women joined the Land Army and tilled the fields and tended the livestock, while others joined the ARP, like those seen here. They went out on fire watch and cajoled residents to keep to the blackout with the well worn cry 'Turn that light out'. They were in the thick of it when the bombs were falling as support was offered to overstretched fire and ambulance crews. There were around 1.4 million ARP wardens in Britain during the war, almost all unpaid part-time volunteers who also held day-time jobs.

Right: During the second world war, the enemy turned its attention to attacking the heart and soul of this country. It had already targeted industry and the nation's infrastructure when it turned its attention to the people living within these shores and that which they held most dear. Centres of population were singled out as homes were flattened almost indiscriminately. The Luftwaffe also indulged in what became known as the 'Baedeker raids'. Taking its nickname from a series of German travel guides, this bombing programme picked out some of the more historic towns and cities for its focus. During the spring of 1942, Exeter, Bath, Canterbury and Norwich all suffered grievously. In the early hours of 29th April 1942, it was York's turn. There was little chance for anyone to take cover as the bombs began to fall just as the warning sirens sounded. A large number of incendiaries and high explosive devices rained down on the city, killing over 70 and injuring more than 200. The Guildhall can be seen here as the flames gutted the historic building. Situated on the east bank of the Ouse, close to where the Romans are thought to have built a bridge, this hall was first used for a public meeting in 1459. After the war the Lord Mayor dedicated its rebuilding to the 'liberation of the world'.

Above: These workmen had the thankless task of making the bomb damaged Bar Convent safe after the assault on it from Herr Goering's squadrons in the spring of 1942. Searching through the rubble was a dangerous and potentially heartbreaking job. There was always the chance that an unexploded bomb might be lying in wait for them and that a sudden movement could set off a delayed detonation. Then there was the effect on the feelings of these workmen as they were never sure what lay beneath the bricks, concrete and glass. Bodies torn apart in the blast could be lying under their feet and no one can calculate the mental anguish they would feel if they unearthed a grisly sight. Some of these men suffered nightmares for years afterwards about their experiences on Nunnery Lane and other similar spots across the city. Newspaper reports were censored but, where they were allowed to report, editors concentrated on the stoicism and heroism of those involved. One even had a report of a pair of swans that continued to nest throughout the carnage around them. It was felt that, had the real story been written, the morale of the general population would be affected. But, word of mouth meant that most of us knew that the true picture was more significant than jolly stories about birds.

The colossal power of the high explosive and its after effect is clearly illustrated in this photograph that shows Bar Convent, or what was left of it after the air raid of 29th April 1942. Rubble and debris lies around everywhere and it is hard now to fully imagine the sheer terror that those caught up in the blast must have felt. The image was captured just six days after the event that illustrated that the innocent were not to be spared the horror of war on the home front. The convent school was just one of several educational establishments that suffered, including Poppleton Road, Queen Anne, the Manor and the Yorkshire School for the Blind. Fortunately, the girls who boarded at the convent had already been led to safety, but the nuns were not so lucky. When the building was first hit, one elderly nun was injured and trapped in the wreckage. Her colleagues went to her assistance but another direct hit killed five of them. The names of those who perished, Mother Vincent (the headmistress), Mother Patricia, Sister Brandon, Mother Agnes and Mother Gerard are on the roll of honour held at heaven's gate.

Bottom: The Women's Voluntary Service was founded as a Civil Defence auxiliary unit in 1938. The WVS gained much experience in providing emergency meals during the second world war, often using the most primitive equipment. WVS mobile canteens served the forces both at home and abroad. During the war years the WVS gained an unforgettable reputation amongst both members of the armed forces and those whose homes had been bombed, always ensuring that cups of tea, sandwiches and cakes were provided exactly where they were needed. When the war ended however members of the WVS had acquired a taste for public service and were unwilling simply to close shop. Distributing Meals on Wheels on a regular basis to needy people, particularly the elderly, after the war was a new challenge, but one the organisation readily adapted to. In the first six months of 1958, the year when this photograph was taken, the WVS delivered 75,000 such meals - the first course always piping hot from 'Hot Lock' containers. In this picture the WVS are looking delighted at the acquisition of two brand new vans. The fully-fitted vehicles named Cowan and Hanover are gaining the seal of approval from two key figures in WVS: standing in front of the bonnet of Hanover are, from right to left, Mrs Marshal the Meals on Wheels organiser for Edinburgh Central, and Lady MacColl, Chairman of WVS Scotland. Things had moved a long way from the immediate post-war years when members often delivered meals in their own vehicles.

Left: War had been declared, and every citizen of Britain, young and old, male and female, was called upon to put his or her back into the war effort. Those who did not go into military service of one kind or another worked in factories, dug for victory, gave up their aluminium baths and saucepans, joined organisations and aided in any way they could. These boys from were not going to be left out; they might be too young to fight but while there were sandbags to be filled they were going to do their bit to protect their school building. Thousands of sandbags were used during World War II to protect the country and its beautiful civic buildings.

Below: It was possibly the acute wartime shortages of food and supplies which made doctors, health workers and mothers alike very aware of the health of the new generation, and children were carefully weighed, measured and immunised against the illnesses that had at one time meant disfigurement or even death. A vaccine for polio, the scourge of former years which left behind its terrible mark of wasted and useless limbs, only came later, however. American scientist Jonas Edward Salk developed a vaccine in 1955, and an oral vaccine was produced in 1960. The vaccines brought the dreaded disease under control and today polio is rarely seen. On a day to day basis, vitamins were vital to the health of children, and long before the advent of the cod liver oil capsule, the recommended spoonful of cod liver oil was administered to the youngest children every day in schools and nurseries around the country during the 1940s. Children might have screwed up their noses at the fishy taste, but the nourishing cod liver oil went a long way towards keeping them healthy. The vitamin-packed orange juice was far more palatable, and artful mothers would often use the orange juice as a bribe: no cod liver oil, no orange juice. Following hard on the heels of the oil, the juice took away the distinctive taste that was disliked by so many children.

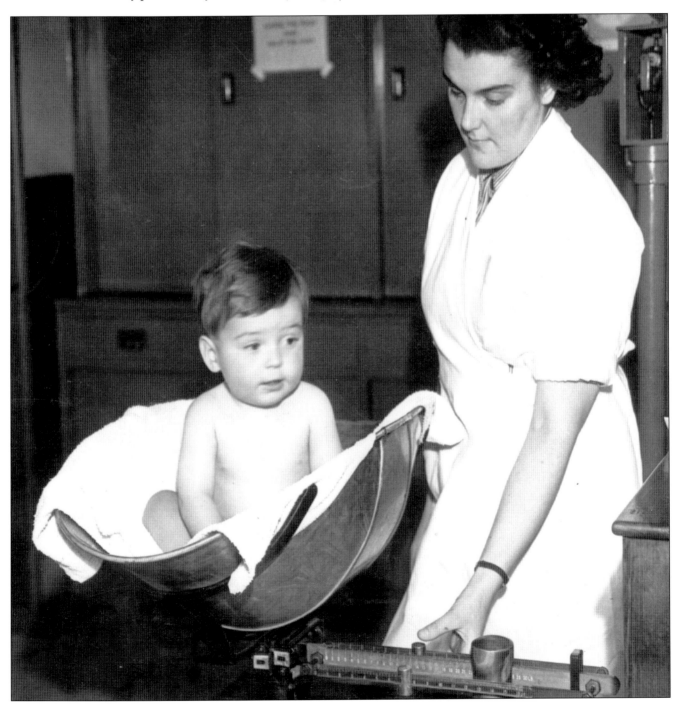

Facing page: In 1939 Britain's Prime Minister Neville Chamberlain had made his announcement to the waiting people of Britain that '...this country is at war with Germany.' The country rolled up its sleeves and prepared for the inevitable. This war would be different from other wars. This time planes had the ability to fly further and carry a heavier load, and air raids were fully expected. Air raid shelters were obviously going to be needed, and shelters were built on open places across towns and cities. By the time war was declared an army of volunteers of both sexes had already been recruited to form an Air Raid Protection service. At first ARP personnel were unpaid volunteers but when war broke out in September 1939 they became paid staff. It was their job to patrol specified areas, making sure that no chinks of light broke the blackout restrictions, checking the safety of local residents, being alert for gas attacks, air raids and unexploded bombs. The exceptional work done by Air Raid Wardens in dealing with incendiaries, giving first aid to the injured, helping to rescue victims from their bombed-out properties, clearing away rubble, and a thousand and one other tasks became legendary; during the second world war nearly as many private citizens were killed as troops - and many of them were the gallant ARP wardens. At the beginning of the war Sir Anthony Eden, Secretary of State for War, appealed in a radio broadcast for men between 17 and 65 to make up a new force, the Local Defence Volunteers, to guard vulnerable points from possible Nazi attack. Within a very short time the first men were putting their names down. At first the new force had to improvise; there were no weapons to spare and men had to rely on sticks, shotguns handed in by local people, and on sheer determination . Weapons and uniforms did not become available for several months. In July the Local Defence Volunteers was renamed the Home Guard, and by the following year were a force to be reckoned with. Television programmes such as 'Dad's Army' have unfortunately associated the Home Guard with comedy, but in fact they performed much important work. The Guard posted sentries to watch for possible aircraft or parachute landings at likely spots such as disused aerodromes, golf courses on the outskirts of towns, local parks and racecourses. They manned anti-aircraft rocket guns, liaised with other units and with regular troops, set up communications and organised balloon barrages. Other preparations were hastily made. Place names and other identifying marks were obliterated to confuse the enemy about exactly where they were. Notices went up everywhere giving good advice to citizens on a number of issues. 'Keep Mum - she's not so dumb' warned people to take care what kind of information they passed on, as the person they were speaking to could be an enemy.

Left: Winston Churchill made a number of morale boosting visits to the provinces during World War II. He had married Clementine Hozier in September 1908. She was a dazzling, but largely penniless beauty whom he met at a dinner party that March. Her background was shrouded in a mixture of mystery and scandal. Officially, her parents were Sir Henry Montague Hozier and Lady Blanche (née Ogilvy). Winston and Clementine had five children and their only son, Randolph, also entered politics. Winston Churchill (1874-1965) had a chequered and varied career, but eventually came to be regarded as one of the most influential Britons that have ever lived. At various times he was an author, soldier, journalist, legislator and painter. A descendant of the Dukes of Marlborough, like so many of his class, Churchill was packed off to boarding school as a youngster and spent an unhappy, lonely time as a youth. After graduating from Sandhurst, he worked as both a soldier and a reporter, but his main love was politics. In 1900, he became Oldham's MP and the love affair with power really began.

EVENTS & OCCASIONS

The Grand Yorkshire Gala on Bootham Field was first held in 1859 and became a much anticipated annual event. It included displays of flowers and fruit, hot air ballooning and a fair.

In this image from the early 1900s, people are making their way in and out of the grounds as a policeman stands by, just in case he is needed to deal with the pickpockets who were something of a nuisance on these occasions.

The tents and marquees where produce was displayed and exhibitions were mounted can be clearly seen. Bootham Hospital, in whose grounds the Gala took place, stands further on. It was built by public subscription in the 1770s as York County Lunatic Asylum. They did not mince their words at that time. Designed by local architect John Carr, it was one of the first psychiatric hospitals in the north of England. It was originally intended to hold 54 patients, but was extended in 1808 when a new wing was added. The Gala was held here until 1934 and helped raise money for local charities. It also gave people a chance to demonstrate their skills in growing fruit, vegetables and flowers. As well as a sense of pride, champion exhibitors could pick up a cash prize ranging from 10 shillings for a nicely displayed bowl of fruit to £20 for a handsome floral display.

Left: Their mothers must have taken an age in getting these girls ready for their part in the York Pageant. Their dresses were carefully chosen and fitted with as much care as might be bestowed upon a modern supermodel. The time taken in garlanding the youngsters' hair so prettily with paper flowers was well spent as they looked a treat as they posed for this portrait, taken on 19th July 1909. Their costumes reflected the craze at the time for classical dancing of a Greek style. The Pageant included various tableaux that reflected many themes, including such diverse ones as Emperor Constantine, King Harold, the marriage of Edward III and Danes and Saxons in Jorvik. Some 2,000 people participated in the event that culminated in an assembled rendition of 'Triumph Song for York', written specially for the occasion by Tertius Noble and James Rhoades. The chorus was split into two parts, one representing memory and the other hope. The Pageant was held in the Museum Gardens and was opened by the Duke of Argyll and Duchess Louise. One of the buglers taking part in a Civil War re-enactment had known proper active service of his own. Corporal Shurlock of the 5th Royal Irish Lancers had sounded the first cavalry charge of the Boer War.

Below: Moss Street, off Blossom Street, was the scene for these peace celebrations in August 1919. Fancy dress was the order of the day and several of the girls seem to have settled on nursing as their theme. One of the boys came as a Red Indian. Perhaps he had been inspired by tales of Buffalo Bill's touring Wild West show that came to Europe in late Victorian times. The celebrations were held on the anniversary of the outbreak of the Great War in 1914. Local councils were responsible for funding the various events, but how many of these children had a relative whose remains lay at Ypres, on the Somme or were just simply missing without trace? This had been the war to end all wars, or so the population had been told. This statement was followed by Lloyd George's declaration that the government would build homes fit for heroes. Fine words, but little in reality. Those who did come back returned to an economically crippled country that would soon plunge into recession that brought the depression years of the 1920s and 1930s. The tots in this photograph would grow into adults with the prospect of high unemployment and low wages to greet them. Worse still, the boys in the picture would go off to battle again in 1939, leaving the girls behind to grieve just as their mothers had done.

Millfield Road, off Scarcroft Road, was bedecked with Union flags and bunting as the peace celebrations of August 1919 got under way. The war had been over since the eleventh hour of the eleventh day of the eleventh month in 1918, something that would be remembered as Armistice Day in future years. This became known as Remembrance Day after the second world war. The mood, while celebratory, on Millfield Road was tinged with sadness at the memory of so many brave men who had fallen during the hostilities that had cost millions of lives. Some recalled the late summer of 1914 when our boys proudly marched off to cries of 'Back by Christmas'. The reality of 20th century warfare was to hit them hard. When the time came by which they had hoped to have returned home, a continuous line of trenches, full of weary soldiers, stretched from the North Sea to Switzerland. Already, 100,000 had been lost at Ypres and the harsh times on the Somme, in Verdun, over the waters in Gallipoli and at Passchendaele lay ahead. It was with a mixture of relief as much as rejoicing that these parties took place. But for every person who cheered the peace, there was another who shed a tear that her Tommy lay somewhere in a foreign field. Lest we forget.

Right: When Edward, Prince of Wales, visited the Rowntree's factory during his visit to the city in 1923, he was presented with a casket of chocolates and an illuminated address from the company's employees. He had been made an honorary Freeman of the City and the visit to the cocoa works was one of a series of engagements lined up for him. As heir to the throne, he was expected to play his part in representing his father, George V, at formal occasions, but there were times that his behaviour left much to be desired. Here, he adopted a bored expression and was obviously a million miles away in his thoughts. Edward, known to his family as David, one of his other names, had developed a reputation for the high life and enjoyed almost film star status in the gossip columns. However, this was not the full picture. He had volunteered to fight in the first world war, but was turned down for security reasons. Despite this, he visited the front lines and was popular with those in the trenches. He reigned as Edward VIII for part of 1936 before abdicating in order to marry the American divorcee and socialite, Wallis Simpson.

Left: On the corner of St Helen's Square and Coney Street, this young scout posed an amusing picture for the cameraman who was keen to have some alternative footage to that of conventional shots of the Prince of Wales' visit on 31st May 1923. A detachment of scouts, cubs and girl guides lined the road opposite the Mansion House, along with several policemen who seemed to be enjoying the fun. These days we have to suffer heavy security measures during a royal visit, but over 80 years ago there was little thought that anyone would wish to launch an assault on such an important personage. Scouting was still quite new in 1923. Just 16 years earlier, Robert Baden-Powell, the hero of the siege of Mafeking during the Boer War, organised a camp for boys on Brownsea Island in Poole Harbour. In 1908 he published 'Scouting for Boys' and the movement took off to such an extent that it rapidly became the world's largest youth movement. It was not long before girls wanted to join but BP, as the founder was known to everyone, resisted the idea. However, with his sister Agnes' help, he began the Girl Guides or Girl Scouts in 1910. The uniform worn by the girls seen here is a far cry from the modern one that Jeff Banks designed in 1990 and was updated in 2000 by Ally Capellino.

Above: During their visit to York in 1925, the Duke and Duchess of York visited the County Hospital and lunched at the Mansion House before going on to York Minster, where the Duchess unveiled the Five Sisters Window and war memorial to the women who gave their lives during the Great War, as it was then known. The medieval glass had been removed from the Minster for safekeeping during the war. A guard of honour was formed by 150 men and women from the North Riding section of the Red Cross, commanded by Major Sir Robert Bower. The Duchess was a beautiful woman and her charm and appeal is well captured in the smile of pleasure on her face. She was a royal who was determined to play a full role in her position in society and she did it with a mixture of responsibility and enjoyment. Born Elizabeth Bowes Lyons in 1900, she would become the best loved of all the 20th century royal figures. She married Prince Albert in 1923, little realising what lay ahead. After his brother's abdication, Albert became George VI and Elizabeth his queen. In later life she became revered as 'Queen Mum'. The Duchess was talking with Lady Bell and we can tell that she clearly had an eye for modern fashion. The cloche hat and ankle revealing dress were quite chic.

Above: Over 80 years ago, women in professions such as nursing and teaching, were expected to devote themselves to their jobs and not divide their loyalties by possessing such distractions as husbands. Spinsterhood meant dedication or, perhaps, it was vice versa. As soon as the altar beckoned, then the exit door from the job was opened. Those rising to the top remained without spousal hindrance. One such example here was the Matron, Miss Steele. She cast a stern glance at the workforce who took their lead from her, just to make sure that everything was just as it should be during the visit of the royal couple. With the Archbishop of York just behind the Duke and Duchess of York, there were more than enough dignitaries for Miss Steele, thank you very much. She tolerated them, even if it did mean that the smooth running of the County Hospital was compromised for a while. If they were not enough, she also had to accommodate John Bickle, Clerk of Works, John J Hunt, the brewer, and the 97 year old Jimmy Melrose, a former Lord Mayor and magistrate. On 24th June 1925, the royals visited several sites in the city, including the County Hospital on Monkgate that was founded in 1740, though this building dates from 1851. It closed in 1977.

Below: Presumably this was the height of public address technology in 1924 as Councillor Watson addressed the crowd who had come along to enjoy the ox roasting and all the fun of the fair on St George's Field. The loaves were piled high at his side, so there must have been plenty of ox to be had to fill all these potential sandwiches. Part of this area has now been given over to a 24 hour car park, but there is still a good expanse of lightly wooded parkland remaining. Up until 1607, female offenders were taken across the field to the river bank and punished by use of a ducking stool. Their crimes ranged from brewing bad beer to accusations of being a scold. All chauvinistic male readers will now do well to refrain from any comments on the rights and wrongs of such ways of meting out retribution for such heinous crimes. In medieval times, citizens had the right to walk, practise their archery or hang out their washing on the field. Much of the original land was lost in the 19th century when Tower Street was constructed. In 1924, these ladies in the picture had no need to fear the ducking stool. They had moved a long way from being part of their husband's estate, as many appeared to be in earlier times. The Great War had given them a voice and an equal part to play in society as they took over male roles in the workplace when their menfolk marched off to war.

Above: Coney Street was gaily decorated with Union flags, bunting and streamers during Civic Week, held on the 17th-23rd June 1928. York celebrated its own existence with a series of processions, parades and exhibitions across the city. There were floral displays aplenty, marching bands to enjoy and a real sense of pride was in the air as we all celebrated our heritage. Parades displayed tableaux that reminded us of our past. They included everything from prehistoric times to the coming of the railways. The celebrations were rounded off with a regatta on the river. One day was given over to a demonstration of our country's importance as a force in the world. Military Sunday showed off the armed forces' latest strength in ordnance and manpower. It was only 10 years since the Great War had been fought and we were still one of the great powers, On 20th June, the fire brigade got an extra practice that it was not expecting. Sparks from the overhead tram cables on Bridge Street set the decorations alight, but fortunately the men from the fire service responded promptly and dealt with the problem before any real damage was suffered. Those watching gave the men three hearty cheers for a job well done.

Right: What a patient race we used to be. Just a couple of bobbies on hand to keep a large crowd in its place was all that was needed. The mounted officer must have brought to mind the famous occasion in 1923 when PC Scorey used his white horse, Billy, to help shepherd nearly 200,000 people who had crammed into Wembley to watch the first FA Cup Final to be played there. The policeman and his noble steed were the epitome of British sang froid on that day. Although the crowd was smaller on St Leonard's Place in June 1928, the approach of the constables was just the same. They dealt with the issue in a professional manner. The spectators played their part. There was no pushing and shoving and the little ones were put to the front where they could get a better view. Little boys in their school uniforms stood alongside small girls in sandals and short white socks. Ladies looked very fashionable in their cloche hats and most of the menfolk wore hats of one sort or another. They were anxious to see the Pageant Procession as it weaved its way through the city. Scenes taken from important times in York's history were enacted as the procession made its way from Dean's Park to the Museum Gardens on three separate occasions during Civic Week.

Above: Terry's on Bishopthorpe Road, Clementhorpe was honoured with a royal visit on 10th October 1937. The company could trace its roots back to 1767 when it was founded as Bayldon and Berry, confectioners. It changed its name in 1828 when Joseph Terry became a partner in the business. It was one of the first companies to concentrate on manufacturing eating rather than drinking chocolate. Sadly, the factory closed in 2005, Kraft having taken over the business 12 years earlier. Production of the renowned Chocolate Orange and All Gold was moved to such unlikely spots as Sweden, Poland and Slovakia. The factory visited by King George VI and Queen Elizabeth was the bees' knees in modern facilities, having only been built in 1926. The royal couple obviously enjoyed their time here as they overstayed their visit, though they certainly did not outstay their welcome. Beatrice Weaver presented a large box of chocolates to the Queen and Lilian Shepherd did likewise to the King's sister, the Princess Royal. The boxes would have taken some getting through as they weighed 8 lbs each. Smaller boxes were handed over for presentation to the young princesses, Elizabeth and Margaret. As the gifts were handed over, we can see that, as usual, the Queen took centre stage as her husband displayed his typical lack of self confidence.

Right: She became known to us all in the second half of her life as our very own 'Queen Mum'. Before that, she was Queen Elizabeth, consort to King George VI and the former Lady Elizabeth Bowes-Lyon. He was inspecting a guard of honour outside Terry's Café at the time, but more people seemed interested in observing the woman who was to be the driving force behind the throne as time went by. A personable and determined woman, Elizabeth was seen on Tuesday 19th October 1937 in company with the Lord Mayor, Thomas Morris, Lord Harewood and the General Commanding Officer in Chief of Northern Command. The party was completed by Mary, Princess Royal and wife of Lord Harewood. Born in 1897, she was just 18 months younger than her brother, the King. During World War I, she visited hospitals and welfare organizations with her mother, Queen Mary, assisting with projects to give comfort to British servicemen and assistance to their families. Later, she took a nursing course and spent some time at Great Ormond Street Hospital. The Princess Royal became the honorary president of the Girl Guide Association in 1920, a role she fulfilled until her death in 1965. Her sister in law, by then, had been a widow for 13 years and later witnessed her own granddaughter, Anne, succeeding Mary as Princes Royal.

Below: The Lord Mayor had departed York in April 1950 on his flag waving trip to America and Canada, leaving his chain of office, valued at £4,325, and his ceremonial robes in the safe hands of WC Caygill. He was the Mansion House butler who was in charge of the day to day running that included ensuring that the office holder had the appropriate garb and necessary impedimenta. He wondered quite how the Mayor would manage without him. The role of this senior local government figure dates back to Norman times. The first mayor was installed in Thetford in 1199. He was acknowledged as the first citizen of the town and had a council for assistance. The mayor was also the custodian of the peace and would preside in the town criminal and civil courts as an early form of magistrate. York's Lord Mayor is second only in precedence to that of London, so this is a most responsible office. Mr Caygill looked quite non-plussed as he stood watching his boss disappear and his pose seems to have amused some of the ladies watching the scene. Their fur stoles and coats would raise an eyebrow or two today among the politically correct, but in the mid 20th century they were a sign of affluence and a badge of importance.

Above: In April 1950, the Lord Mayor JB Morrell inspected the troops from the Duke of Wellington Regiment who were lined up in Tea Room Square. He was accompanied by Captain Ormsby as he prepared to set off across the Atlantic on a good will trip to America and Canada. Morrell was accompanied on this venture by the Sheriff and they stayed at the home of the brother of Councillor Leramouth in New York during part of the visit. The Lord Mayor took a replica of the official chain of office with him as the original was too valuable to risk on such a lengthy journey. He also did without his robes in order to keep the baggage weight down. The 10,000 mile round trip was meant to promote York and invite people from across the big pond to join in the celebrations for the Festival of Britain, planned for the following year. This nationwide jamboree was the brainchild of the Labour government that saw it as a way to mark the centenary of the Great Exhibition and lift public morale during the austere postwar years. However, many came to question the cost of the festivities that included the erection of the Skylon, a floodlit form of an aluminium exclamation mark floating above London. Some wags likened it to Clement Attlee as it had no visible support!

TRANSPORT

York has been a centre of transport developments for at least 2,000 years - and probably much longer. Few modes of transport however have lasted such a short period of time yet been missed so much than York's trams. State of the art electric trams made their first appearance in the city in 1910. Yet by only 1935 they were history. Poor technology? Not at all. Just simple economics: overhead power cables and special tracks took much more money to build and maintain than did roads on which trolley-busses, and motor buses, could travel alongside cars and lorries. Passengers in his 1920s photograph however would not have been likely to have realised that the tram's days were numbered. Still less would they have imagined that large centres such as Sheffield and Manchester would one be putting trams back on their streets every bit as enthusiastically as they once ripped them out.

Above: Parked on Deangate, this 1921 ambulance was stationary outside the Minster. St Michael Le Belfrey Church is to the left. It looks a bizarre sight to those of us used to the well equipped, paramedic centres on wheels of the 21st century, but this is how our grandparents were transported to the local infirmary. The modern ambulance service developed as a result of the 1946 National Health Services Act when local authorities were required to provide ambulances 'where necessary'. Prior to then the chance of being transferred to hospital in an ambulance depended upon where you lived. Ambulances were mostly available in cites and large towns and were initially staffed by volunteers transporting the sick and injured to hospital for treatment. Professionals were gradually introduced and in 1964 the Millar report recommended that the ambulance service should provide treatment in addition to transporting patients. This echoed the attitude expressed in a leader in the Times newspaper in 1832 during a cholera outbreak in London when it suggested that curative treatment should begin during transportation to hospital. Horse drawn ambulances were used throughout the 19th century until the advent of the automobile engine. The use of motorised ambulances, similar to this civilian one, helped save many lives at the front in World War I, but the emphasis was still on transportation rather than life saving.

Above right: Reo Young sat proudly at the wheel of her 1930s' version of Del Boy's favoured mode of transport half a century later. The Ankers Garage on Gillygate was the sole agent in the area for the James van. At 100 guineas (£105), it did not come cheap, considering that the average man in the street was pleased if he got a fiver a week in wages. However, it did have one advantage in the cost of motoring. Its fuel consumption was good and, because it sat upon a motorbike chassis and did not possess a reverse gear, the annual road tax was lower than that of a conventional car or small van. Like many other businesses before, the James Company was formerly a cycle manufacturer. It launched the 5 cwt Handy van in 1929, using a 247 cc motorcycle engine. This was a little underpowered and continual updates and modifications over the next few years saw the introduction of the 'Samson' Handy van in 1933. This powered by an air-cooled, v-twin 1,096cc engine and had an aluminium body and a new welded steel frame chassis. The James Company ceased trading in 1939, but some other three wheelers lasted much longer. Amongst the most famous of these is the Morgan brand that began in Malvern in 1910. The Trotters' Reliant Robin is a more recent machine, first manufactured in 1973.

originally a Huddersfield firm, founded by Herbert and Reginald Clayton. It began car manufacture in 1908, but began to concentrate on commercial vehicles after the first world war. It produced such varied vehicles as dustcarts, tractors to haul road trailers for the railways, trucks and buses. The company was taken over by Rootes in 1934 and the Huddersfield plant closed. By then, the trolley bus was also on its way out. It had helped kill off the tram, but was also found to be superfluous to the city's transport needs. The first vehicle ran on 22nd December 1922, but by 5th January 1935 the motor bus had taken over all the routes. Bradford and Leeds introduced the first trolley buses in 1911 and they were particularly useful in hilly areas that diesel or

Below: This Karrier Clough trolley bus was one of three of its type that entered service on 6 October 1931. Bound for Heworth, this one was passing 115 East Parade, opposite Second Avenue. Trolley buses helped toll the death knell for the trams. They were easier to maintain and expensive tracks could be dispensed with. Karrier was petrol driven buses found difficult before improved technology enhanced their specifications. They were clean and relatively quiet vehicles, though so smoothly did they run that some people referred to them as the 'whispering death' as they caught pedestrians crossing the street unawares.

Below: Trams in York had only got another 12 months' service left in them when this scene on Museum Street was recorded in 1934. Their demise was as a result of the greater flexibility of the motor buses similar to the one about to overtake the car that was on its way to South Bank. The overtaking manoeuvre looks a little hairy as the bus driver was sweeping past on a bend. At this time, road safety was quite a contentious issue in Britain. We had one of the worst records in Europe for the number of accidents and fatalities on our highways. Electrically controlled traffic lights were still relatively new and the Highway Code had not long been written. Just about anyone could jump behind the wheel and it was only now that a driving test was established that forced new motorists to have their abilities examined by trained inspectors. Even so, established drivers were exempted from the test and, in many cases, people who had little road experience could still bypass the formalities. The introduction of further safety measures, such as Halifax man Percy Shaw's cats' eyes and the Belisha crossing, did help. Better street lighting made night driving somewhat safer and, eventually, safety education in schools with the 'Stop, look and listen' programme and cycle proficiency schemes gave the future driving generation a better understanding.

Above: At the start of the last century there were just 11 trams in the city, drawn by horses from a pool of 38. The animals were withdrawn by 1909 as electrification of the tramway was phased in. Compared with many other towns and cities, the electric tram's length of service was relatively short, spanning little more than a quarter of a century. Even so, there was an affection for it as it marked a major move in the then modern technology. The harnessing of electricity was a powerful tool in the development of our everyday lives. The humble tram was even immortalised in film and music when Judy Garland performed 'The Trolley Song' in the movie 'Meet me in St Louis'. The open cars were draughty vehicles and none too popular with locals during inclement weather. The one in the foreground was on the run from Acomb to Lindley Street and was photographed on Queen Street Bridge. The No 45 behind was a former Burton on Trent tram. The Railway Institute can be seen in the background. York's last tram ran on Saturday, 16th November 1935, a year or so after this photograph was taken. On that final day, large crowds gathered at midnight to witness the final journey from Nessgate. The Lord Mayor and Inspector JA Stewart were at the controls, the latter being the driver of the very same car that had run at the service's official opening.

Below: Author Kenneth Grahame (1859-1932) is best remembered for his 1908 book 'Wind in the Willows'. The driver of this 1933 car might just have been modelled on Mr Toad. It is certainly the type of tourer that would have got the old boy's heart racing, as well as the engine. He would happily speed along the lanes, shouting 'What fun!' and fun it must have been in real life for the owner of such a car. Britain's roads were not cluttered with traffic as they became later on and it was easy to find an open stretch of road and just let rip. This fine example of craftsmanship, registered in 1933, was observed on Heworth Hall Drive outside some of the recently built houses. Heworth Moor has a niche in history as it was the scene of a skirmish on 24th August 1454 between the Percy and Neville families. This is thought by many historians to be the first military encounter in the Wars of the Roses. Younger readers might look at the front of the car and observe a small hole at the bottom of the radiator grille and wonder as to its use. This was where a starting handle was inserted and the engine cranked over if the so called self starting button or interior switch did not succeed in stirring the car into life.

Above: Heworth village takes its name from the Anglo Saxon for 'enclosure', though the area has links with Roman times as Heworth Green is on the site of a road dating back almost 2,000 years. Situated about a mile from the city centre, the village has grown over the last century to become one of the surrounding ring of suburbs. New housing in the 1930s included the creation of Heworth Hall Drive and similar estates. This one was still to be completed when the Ankers and Young families posed for this photograph. They were related by marriage and involved in the motor trade and garage business. The original Hall was a handsome villa, built in 1830. The house and accompanying 12 acres of prime building land were sold at auction in 1928. Builders Sherry, Temple and Caffrey put up housing here and on Walney Road. Heworth Hall was demolished in 1934, but its coach house was retained and more recently used by the Seventh Day Adventist Church. This group gathered near No 31 Heworth Hall Drive and would have been one of those upwardly mobile families of the interwar years who had done well in business and was now happy to enjoy the comfort of a new home with all the mod cons that perhaps their parents had missed out on.

SHOPPING SPREE

Goodramgate runs from Holy Trinity Church, north towards the city wall and the Richard III Museum at Monk Bar. There are a number of good restaurants along here today, but in this photograph taken during the second world war the focus is on general retail. Mattison's hairdresser's, on the left, is from where a fashionable young woman of the era could emerge looking like one of the Andrews Sisters. Minton's paints and varnish shop

was on the other side of the road, while further down we can see Tom Wood the butcher, Nutbrown the fruiterer, Webster's shoe shop, William Wright the butcher, Dacre's drapery and John Saville the chemist. These indicate the variety of establishments that flourished along Goodramgate once over. In this period, though, several struggled to make ends meet. Rationing was quite severe and the amount of food each family could buy was heavily restricted. Even clothing was hard to come by and everybody had to mend and make do. Just a solitary car was on the road and people got about under their own steam, or by getting bikes that had not been used since the mid 1930s out from the shed. The cyclist on the left was passing the Golden Slipper public house. It was a medieval tradition to place two shoes in the construction of a building to ward off evil spirits and a slipper was found by workmen here in 1984 during refurbishment.

Hunter and Smallpage, on the right of this World War II photograph, was a high class furniture and soft furnishings shop at 57 Goodramgate. The firm also diversified into designing school shields and plaques for family 'coats of arms'. Concentrating more on carpets and flooring, the company is now based on Micklegate. The odd looking vehicle on the right belonged to London North East Railways. This three wheeler, with a detachable trailer, was used as a delivery van and was one of the range of vans, trucks and lorries manufactured by Scammell. Originally wheelwrights and carriage makers in Victorian times, the company switched to the production of lorries in 1921. It also developed tractors, tank transporters and troop carriers that were more than useful during the war. The company ceased production in 1988. Looking towards Deangate, the buildings on the left included the Peter Rabbit Wool Shop, Ye Olde Cake Shoppe, Home and Colonial Grocery and the Phitwell tailor's shop. This latter establishment used a neat play on words in an age when bespoke tailoring had come under challenge from the ready to wear chains. Before rationing bit hard, the likes of Burton and Price's the Fifty Shilling Tailor had threatened the livelihood of the made to measure market. This trend continued after the war when ex-servicemen ignored the likes of Phitwell for their demob suits.

Below: The soldier walking towards the camera in 1940 was possibly on leave from his duties in the armed forces. Perhaps he was one of those who had been evacuated from Dunkirk in the flotilla of boats, both large and small, that helped save the bacon of thousands of our men who were stranded on the shores of northern France as the enemy attempted to wipe out an army that had been pushed all the way back to the coast. Without the bravery of those who set sail across the Channel in late May and early June to take part in Operation Dynamo, we would have lost the bulk of our expeditionary forces. The large Rover in the centre of Feasegate, pointing towards St Sampson's Square, packed 13.9 horsepower under its bonnet. It was a far cry from the first Rover, a tricycle built in 1883 by Starley and Sutton. The company was renamed the Rover Cycle Company in the late 1890s before switching to motor manufacture with the Rover eight in 1904. This pictured model belonged to Colonel Innes Ware, the City Coroner. A slogan on the van on the right encouraged us to 'Go on buying savings certificates' as part of the war effort. The various retail outlets on the left included Woodcock's confectioners, Hollywood Fashion Shoes, Feasegate Restaurant, Halford's, and Bullivant's fish, game and poultry dealership. The King's Head pub, in the distance, closed in 1958.

Above: The two soldiers heading past the Picture House on Coney Street were probably enjoying a few days' leave in 1940 before they were sent off again to do battle with Herr Hitler's Nazi troops. Deanna Durbin was starring in 'Spring Parade', but the men did not wish to stop off and take in this rather girly tosh about a baker's assistant who falls for a prince. The star, though, was a big name at this time. Still only 19, Durbin had appeared in several films and gained an international following that included Anne Frank. The teenage diarist, who died in a concentration camp, had the actress's picture on her bedroom wall at her home. The Picture House was designed by Albert Winspear and could seat around 1,000 patrons. It opened on 12th April 1914, showing 'When East Meets West'. It had a café restaurant and, in keeping with most similar establishments, its own orchestra. It was bought by Provincial Cinema Theatres in 1919 and taken over by Gaumont-British in 1929. It closed in 1955 after showing 'Prize of Gold', a film that featured young British actors, George Cole and Andrew Ray. After the cinema was demolished the site was used to extend Woolworth's. Across the street, the Montague Burton store at No 52 is now occupied by Fraser Hart. Further down from the Picture House were F Coleridge's ladies' outfitter, the Willow Café and the Fifty Shilling Tailor.

Below: The buildings in the distance on Fossgate are no more. They were cleared in the 1950s to make way for The Stonebow and included the George Hotel and Geoffrey's Photographers. The double gabled, timber framed shop is Thomas Herbert's house. It has been occupied by many businesses over the years, including Curry's Cycle and TV shop, Clark's Shoes and Jones' Shoes. The house was bought in 1557 from the Merchant Adventurers' Company by Thomas' grandfather, Christopher Herbert. He paid the unusual amount of £54 10s 8d (£54.53) for it. Sir Thomas Herbert was appointed to look after Charles I during his imprisonment and was with him at his execution. The king handed Herbert his cloak as he was led to the scaffold in Whitehall in 1649. The house began to look rather weary as time went by and a Birmingham architect, Francis Yorke, was commissioned to restore it to its former glory. He drew up plans in 1924 and completed the work two years later. At the time of the restoration the house was in use as a draper's shop with a warehouse in the building at the rear in Lady Peckitt's Yard. Joseph Rowntree opened a grocery shop on Pavement in 1842. The family had no connection with chocolate or cocoa for another 20 years.

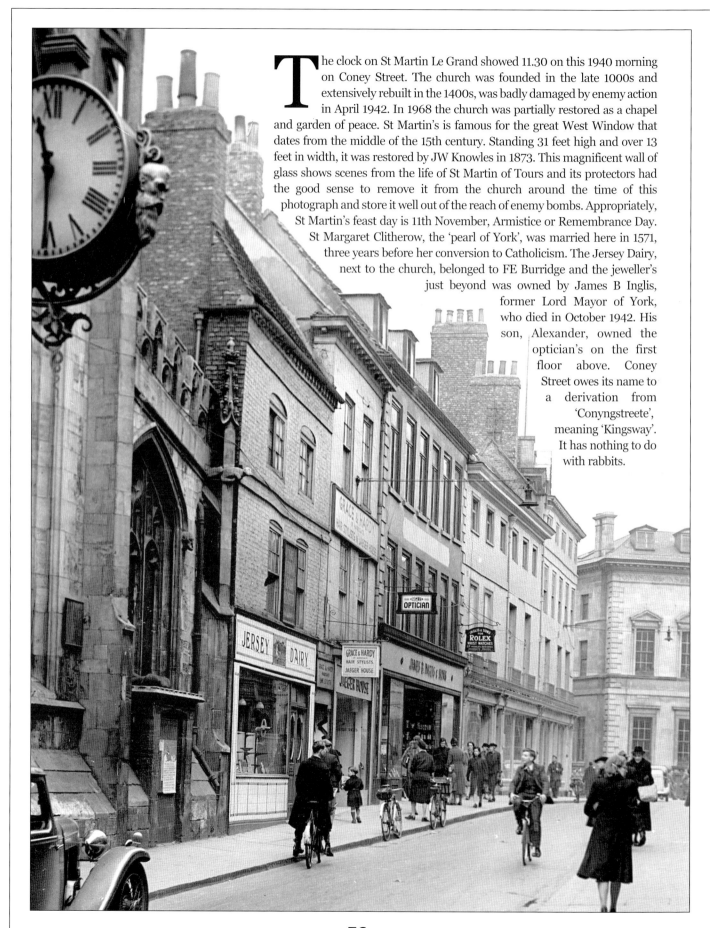

The clock on St Martin Le Grand showed 11.30 on this 1940 morning on Coney Street. The church was founded in the late 1000s and extensively rebuilt in the 1400s, was badly damaged by enemy action in April 1942. In 1968 the church was partially restored as a chapel and garden of peace. St Martin's is famous for the great West Window that dates from the middle of the 15th century. Standing 31 feet high and over 13 feet in width, it was restored by JW Knowles in 1873. This magnificent wall of glass shows scenes from the life of St Martin of Tours and its protectors had the good sense to remove it from the church around the time of this photograph and store it well out of the reach of enemy bombs. Appropriately, St Martin's feast day is 11th November, Armistice or Remembrance Day. St Margaret Clitherow, the 'pearl of York', was married here in 1571, three years before her conversion to Catholicism. The Jersey Dairy, next to the church, belonged to FE Burridge and the jeweller's just beyond was owned by James B Inglis, former Lord Mayor of York, who died in October 1942. His son, Alexander, owned the optician's on the first floor above. Coney Street owes its name to a derivation from 'Conyngstreete', meaning 'Kingsway'. It has nothing to do with rabbits.

Below: Seen from Nessgate, the cars were lined up on High Ousegate in the late 1940s. GW Harding's delightful linen and furnishings store was one of the attractions on this street until its closure in 1974. During the 1939-45 War, large signs were put up on some of the buildings in the street directing people to the air raid shelters. Those on High Ousegate just after the last shots had been fired in anger must have wondered what the future held for them. They had come through the deprivation and destruction of six war torn years, but now there was a peace to be won. The country was virtually bankrupt and soon would be in hock to the Americans who offered aid under the Marshall Plan in an effort to bail out their allies and stem the spread of communism. It was to be a debt that hung like a millstone for another 60 years. All around them, ordinary people started to take stock of what they could see and started to ask the question, 'Who really are the winners?' It did not seem to be us. Food, petrol and clothing were all still in short supply and rationing would continue for years to come. Men returning from the front were greeted by children who regarded them as strangers and wives who had learned to get along without them. The Empire was breaking up and a time of uncertainty and austerity lay ahead.

Above: Before its move to Newgate, the market on St Sampson's Square was busy with large numbers of shoppers weaving their way in and out of the cars and lorries that were also trying to wend their way through this crowded spot. The distinctive shape of the Standard Vanguard on the left is easy to identify. The car was introduced in July 1947 and was completely new, with no resemblance to previous models, and was Standard's first postwar car. The company was founded in Coventry in 1903 by RW Maudslay and continued in its own right until 1963, though it had come under the umbrella of Leyland motors in 1960. The Vanguard is approaching a Triumph Renown, a 2 litre model manufactured between 1949 and 1952. Coincidentally, Triumph had been taken over by Standard in 1945. Next to the Standard vehicle, the ice cream van was doing good business and this was no surprise. The owner, J Questa, was of Italian origin, having come to York at the start of the century, and built a fine reputation for his excellent product. His ices sold, if not like hot cakes, then like - -well, ice creams. Questa also had a shop on the corner of St Andrewgate and King's Square.

Below: The 60s do not look very swinging in this photograph, but it is to that era that the image belongs. It was a little early for mini skirts and boys with long, shoulder length hair as this was September 1961, but they would arrive in a few short years' time. Shoppers in Newgate Market might have been humming John Leyton's haunting 'Johnny Remember Me', but two years later it would be all 'She Loves You' and 'yeah-yeah-yeah'. The transfer of the market from Parliament Street was gradual. The fish stalls opened in 1955, but the general market was not fully up to speed until April 1964. In this market scene we can pick out GO Young's fruit and flower stall. Elsewhere, a chicken could be bought for 10 shillings (50p) and haddock was available for 2s 4d (12p) per pound. No one ever dreamed that stallholders would be told to price their goods at metric weights. The stall to the left sold seamless nylons at a couple of bob, or 10p to those readers who are post 1971. These brought back memories of the war to older shoppers. They recalled when such stockings were so scarce that they gravy browned their legs and drew a seam down them with a pencil.

Above: Stonegate was pedestrianised in 1971 and not long after here we see shoppers enjoying the freedom of moving along the road without the petrol fumes and dangers associated with motor cars in the city centre. A couple of cyclists weaving their way through the crowds, though, meant that pedestrians could not relax completely, but it was better than dodging a Renault 16 weaving along the highway. During the 15th and 16th centuries most of the land here belonged to the Minster. Some of it was given to prebends to build houses for their priors, abbots and monks to live in while on business at the Minster. A prebend was a type of canon who had an administrative role at the Minster. During cathedral services they would sit in specially reserved seats, usually at the back of the choir stalls. The large timbered house on the right had been used by of the Bishop of Chester. Long established owners of antique shops on Stonegate remembered the days of royal visits before the war when George V's wife, Queen Mary, used to be a regular visitor whenever in the city. She felt that her patronage of a shop was reward enough and chose a number of expensive items for use in one of the royal palaces, but never offered payment. Wise dealers took to moving their best items out of sight whenever they heard that she was in the vicinity.

Right: Stonegate was very crowded with shoppers who were enjoying the sunshine of an August afternoon in 1978. The hairdresser, just above the Punch Bowl Inn, was happy to offer modern styling that reflected the mood of the times. The Purdy was a popular cut. This was inspired by the character played by Joanna Lumley on the popular television show, 'The New Avengers'. It was hardly brand new fashion, but the association with the glamorous actress helped its promotion. Perhaps we can see a few examples on Stonegate, if we look hard enough. The Purdy has been described as a blunt cut, almost bowl shaped, with a line that angles along the sides to the nape of the neck. This is slightly tapered to curve inward toward the head and give a smooth look to the finished style. It is also sometimes referred to as a mop-top. This latter part of the description puts us in mind of male fads and fancies, because it was the Beatle cut in the 1960s that had young men rushing to unisex salons for the first time as they tried to ape their heroes from Merseyside. Things in the tonsorial world were about to change in 1978 as this was the punk rock era. Soon our streets would see some outlandish coiffeurs being paraded, with shocking pink locks clashing with shaved heads.

AT WORK

The City of York Tramways Company began a programme of expansion and electrification in 1909. An electric tram service was opened from Fulford to the city centre line in January 1910 and relatively quickly after the line from the city centre to Dringhouses was electrified. Subsequently a new route by way of the New Railway Station followed. A short spur to Holgate Bridge and the Haxby Road and Acomb routes were constructed at the same time. (Pictured on the left are a group of men working on the lines for the new electric tram in 1910, and are shown here on The Mount). Lines were opened from the New Railway Station to South Bank in 1913, and along Hull Road in 1916 when the Haxby Road line was also extended. Having rejected an offer of Thomas Tilling to run petrol-electric buses in the city in 1909, the trams were not challenged by buses again until 1914. At this time sanction was given to the corporation to introduce both motor- and trolley-buses, and by 1921 it was necessary to supplement the tram depot which had been built at Fulford in 1880 with a bus depot in Piccadilly. From 1929 onwards all the corporation services increasingly felt the competition of private bus companies which served new suburbs beyond the limit of the tramways. In 1934 a joint committee of the corporation and the West Yorkshire Road Car Company was established to operate services within the city and on a number of routes outside. After 1935 these services were provided by buses alone: the trolley-buses were withdrawn in January and the trams in November that year.

Below: The River Ouse was a major navigation and the number of boats in this picture illustrates its importance to the life of the city. On the left T. Varey and Sons were agricultural merchants and ham and bacon factors. They occupied premises at 17 Skeldergate. The large building on the left behind Ouse Bridge was, at the time, occupied by Varvill and Sons who were saw and tool manufacturers. They had a foundry by the river on the site currently occupied by York Rowing Club

Left: This is the Lozenge Department at Terry's, probably in the early years of the twentieth century. The picture was taken outside the Starch Room. We believe that included in this photo are two people named Frank. At the age of 12 or 13, Frank Lowther started working for the firm in 1889 and retired in 1941 aged 65. Francis (Frank) Sanderson, who would have been about 14 in this photo, worked for Terry's, apart from service in the war, until he migrated in 1967.

Below and right: This doughty trio of Edwardian enforcement was photographed c1908 as it guarded the Minster. The men were part of what is said to be the world's oldest police force, with links as far back as the 13th century. Today, it is very small, specialised constabulary responsible for policing the Minster and its immediate precincts. Its members understand that they are part of a unique and time-honoured body of men, who for hundreds of years have taken care of this magnificent cathedral. They are currently based in an office just off the North Choir Aisle that is marked by

two old-fashioned truncheons hanging next to the door. Originally, the men were known as Constables of Liberty and had a role similar to that of a parish constable. Following an arson attack in 1829, the care of the building was given greater priority, though it was not until 1855 that the title of Minster Police was first used. Robert Peel is said to have observed their work when formulating plans for creating the British police force. Pictured here are Constable Isaac Ankers, Sergeant Morley and Constable Helps. Ankers was known as the 'Minster Beacon' because of his large, red nose. The cause of its colouration was the subject of gossip relating to his liking for an odd draught or two, but it would not be polite to dwell upon that.

This wartime view of Stonegate shows a man working at the top of a set of ladders - probably cleaning windows, as there is a handcart in the street below. There are several pedestrians in the street. Signs include, on the left, an 'S' indicating the site of an air-raid shelter and Margaret Perry's Dressmaking business. On the right there is a paintseller, a hairdresser and Spink's Typewriters. The most impressive shop front is that of W.F. Greenwoods at no. 37 - the antique dealers on the right. This old firm was established in 1829 in High Ousegate as upholsterers, paperhangers and undertakers. When Greenwoods moved to these premises in 1851 it was as cabinet makers and dealers in "ancient furniture". The royal warrant proudly displayed over the door reflects the patronage of the firm, in the first half of the 20th century, by Queen Mary, a notorious "visitor" of antique shops. Many dealers dreaded her descending upon their shops since she had a reputation for "honouring" proprietors of the finest antique shops by requiring the best items on display to be sent to one of her palaces but never making any payment for them. Some dealers reputedly resorted to hiding their finest stock when they knew she was visiting the area, for fear of losing it to this most discerning of patrons. It was said that the Queen similarly honoured her hosts when she stayed at private houses, bestowing her praise on the finest pieces and being mortally offended if they were not consequently offered to her as gifts.

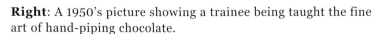

Above: Workers chocolate packing in the Rowntree premises at Haxby Road in York, around 1910.

Left: This image shows a Rowntree's sweet jar containing clear gums and fruit pastilles. Rowntree's had concentrated on cocoa and had a conservative attitude to development until a Monsieur Gaget brought samples of pastilles and showed how cheap the equipment and manufacture could be. In 1881 he succeeded in devising a recipe that satisfied Rowntree's and production began. As a result the workforce doubled between 1880 and 1883 and in 2001 Rowntree's Fruit Pastilles had sales of £46 million.

Right: A 1950's picture showing a trainee being taught the fine art of hand-piping chocolate.

Above: Quite what the Humber lifeboat was doing on the Ouse in the early 1930s is not clear, but we can identify its location as it passed Robert Rook's corn and grain business at 20 Skeldergate. The boat's base was at Spurn Point, from where a succession of craft has sailed since 1810. The station is now the only one in the United Kingdom which has full-time paid staff. York's principal river has a rather boring name. Ouse quite simply means 'water', so we are looking at the uninspiringly titled River Water! It is formed by the confluence of the Ure and Swale rivers in central North Yorkshire. It flows on to Goole and joins the Trent near the Humber Estuary. In the 18th and early 19th centuries, the Ouse was busy, particularly with commercial traffic coming down from Selby, where there was a customs house. However, the opening of the Aire and Calder Navigation in 1826 saw most of the movement head off to Goole. When this photograph was taken, Britain was struggling its way through the depression years. Unemployment was high and the dream of a land fit for heroes that Lloyd George had promised over a decade earlier had never materialised. In a few years' time the lads in short trousers seen here would be pulling on uniforms as the call to arms came again.

Right: Perhaps this photograph from 1978 could be given the headline 'Home on the range'. Quite what the infant is doing behind the chip shop counter is a mystery. Perhaps he was about to be baptised with a drop or two of vinegar to wet his forehead. The women gathered around demonstrated all the usual maternal instincts and cooed and aahed appropriately, while the proprietor looked on a little hesitantly and the male customer thought to himself that he hoped the little perisher was not going to be sick all over his fish supper. Fortunately, the child was well out of the way when the public health inspectorate called to check the premises. They did not find anything untoward such as mouse droppings and gave the shop a tick in all the right columns. Goodness knows what they would have done if they had spotted a dirty nappy in the corner. The humble chippy had enough to cope with at this time. It had reigned supreme in the fast food business for over a century. Fried fish shops were popular in London in the early 19th century, as were fried potatoes in southern Scotland and northern England. Many places claim to have had the first one to sell a combination of both foods, with Oldham's Tommyfield Market being the most favoured. However, the first recorded shop was Malin's in London. By the date of this picture, McDonald's and the rest were major threats to our national institution.

Above: A 1950's view of workers arriving by bus at the Terry's factory on Bishopthorpe Road. As you might expect, the workers in this picture are overwhelmingly female and headscarfs are definitely the order of the day. Terry's, established in York in 1767, moved to these premises in 1925. It was suggested that from the roof of the factory on a clear day, it was possible to see the Pennines which are 45 miles away.

Above: We are a nosy set of people. If there is ever anything slightly out of the ordinary you can be sure that a crowd will gather just to see what is going on. This car was being winched out of the Ouse in 1978 and a knot of onlookers quickly assembled even though no one there had any real interest in the proceedings. It was just something to gawp at and fill in a few idle moments. If the ghoulish among the spectators thought that there was a body inside, then they were to be disappointed. The Ouse has had a more important part to play in York's development through history than being a mere depository for motor vehicles. Formed by the confluence of the Ure and Swale near Boroughbridge, it has a system of tributaries that include the Aire, Derwent, Don, Wharfe, Rother, Nidd and Foss that drain large upland areas of the Yorkshire Dales and Moors. As the Ouse valley is wide and flat, seasonal flooding occurs on a regular basis, bringing major problems to the city and its surrounding areas. Both the Romans and the Vikings found the river an attractive and convenient means of approaching the city from the North Sea. Tidal factors were of the utmost importance to the commercial life of the city. Such is the strength of the tides in the lower Ouse that in the days before steam, a boatman had but two options: to go with the flow or to wait for the turn of the tide.

Wrights of Crockey Hill - Nothing Beyond Our Reach

A few miles outside York, on the Selby Road, is Crockey Hill. There can be found the bustling business of Wrights Plant & Skip Hire.

Wrights of Crockey Hill Ltd is one of the greatest success stories in the competitive world of local business.

Douglas Wright, better known to all who knew him as Doug, founded the business in 1952. After leaving the Army he had gone into market gardening at Cliffe, near Selby, but he then moved into the motor trade, establishing himself at Crockey Hill.

At Crockey Hill Doug set about developing the site, building a new garage behind an existing building. He also had a garage in Selby and another at Holme on Spalding Moor run by his nephew Arthur Hall.

Developing the business even further Doug now moved into agricultural contracting, and introduced combine harvesters, which he both hired out and sold.

Plant hire began in 1960 when the Council was doing some road repairs outside the garage. Doug told the road menders they needed a JCB and went out and bought one which he then hired to the Council.

Doug's nephew Alan Wright joined the firm in 1963 to work on the agricultural contracting side of the business. Buying another JCB to add to the original one. The firm moved on from there to Civil Engineering, suppliers of farm machinery, oil, fuels and even a hotel at Escrick. By 1995 the company had 75 employees. In the early days Wrights employed just seven or eight staff, one of whom being Doug's stepdaughter Susan Wharram who ran the office until 1964 when her successor June Craven took over and continued running the office until 2005.

Another stalwart of the company was Mick Haw, he started as a machine driver, but moved up to run the contracting side of the business as it was expanding, working with local Drainage Boards clearing lake's and ponds, as well as excavating York's Naburn Marina.

Doug was MD until he passed away in 2003.

In 2004 the Company was taken over by Doug's nephew Alan Wright, with Geraldine Lindsay in charge of Company Administration.

Today the firm's main customers include not only local authorities, but also the rail industry and British Waterways.

Alan is already looking to expand the business and proving to be just as successful as his uncle!

*Above: Founder Douglas Wright at the Crockey Hill premises in the early days. **Below left:** Wrights Holme garage in the 1950s. **Below:** Wrights staff photograph, 2007.*

Hogg The Builder
Building Individual Homes of Distinction

Formed in 1968, this privately owned family-run company has established a reputation for building individual new homes of distinction in sought after village locations throughout the Vale of York. An unrelenting attention to detail in every aspect from land acquisition, design and construction, through to completion and after sales service, makes the company's new homes unrivalled.

Company founder Mike Hogg believed "House buyers recognise and appreciate quality. My aim is to build houses that people will enjoy living in".

Mike Hogg set out with an unusual philosophy. Volume house building was not for him – he wanted to build individual homes with charm and

character for his customers. A good reputation, creating a sense of community, and utilising the skills of local craftsmen were all part of that philosophy rather than simply maximising profit which motivated so many other builders.

Mike Hogg started his working life in the 1960s as an apprentice joiner at HJ Bailey, Bishop Wilton, near Garrowby Hill. He subsequently left Bailey's to work for a company in York, Jack Bradley, a large house builder, but that firm subsequently closed. At the age of 24 and without a job Mike decided to start his own business.

Above: *Founder Mike Hogg sole trading as Hogg the Builder in the early days.* **Below:** *The Company's office at Strensall in the 1990's.*

The fledgling firm's first site was at Appleton le Street and consisted of a chalet bungalow which was sold for just over £5,000. Two years later Les Forster, who was also a joiner and had worked with Mike at HJ Bailey, came to join him. Initially they worked on property repairs, small school and local authority work.

Together they established Trustspan Timber Engineering Ltd, a company specialising in the manufacture of roof trusses and timber frames for houses. Both Hogg and Trustspan continued to grow and their progress was inextricably linked in the 1970's and 1980's. The companies initially shared premises at Clifton, York before moving to a large purpose built facility at Brecks Lane, Strensall; which would subsequently become the location of the landmark "Redmayne" development and the site of Hogg's head office, where they remain to this day.

By 1973 Hogg the Builder had established its name with its unique mews-house development at Burnholme. Since then the company has only worked in the areas around York using local knowledge and experience to create homes of quality and character. In the early 1970s Hogg was at the forefront of building timber-framed houses, built in villages south of York at Wistow and Cawood and subsequently re-emerging in 2003 at Orchard End, Hemingbrough with the process now termed "modern methods of construction".

The firm began to build a unique style of home; the 'Dalesman' complete with inglenook fireplaces, solid

Top left: At work on timber frame housing. ***Above:*** *Hogg's Dalesman Cottage range with inglenook fireplace (inset).* ***Below:*** *Neighbours Evening. When a site is completed and all customers have moved in the company invite them all to a local venue for light refreshments so they can all meet and get to know one another.*

exposed beams and distressed stained woodwork throughout. These new homes had the appearance of old and rustic homes, but with all the amenities and advantages that a new house can offer. Two of these cottage style homes, the 'Leyburn' and 'Malham', received extensive coverage in the press at this time.

In 1985, with a growing reputation and a keen ambition to do much more, Mike Hogg conceived the idea of Harton Woods near Flaxton which would be one of several super villages planned for the outskirts of York. The principle features would be housing areas as well as fine new recreational areas. Due to changes in local policy these super villages never came to fruition.

However Mike Hogg's vision for this site has materialised in the form of Sandburn Hall Golf Club, Tykes Restaurant and Griffon Forest luxury holiday

Above: Mike Hogg views the landscape for his vision of a super village at Harton Woods. **Below left:** In 2005 James Hogg opened Sandburn Hall Golf Club in memory of his father, Mike Hogg 'A tribute to his remarkable vision'. **Below and inset:** Sandburn Hall, the largest natural green oak timber framed building since the Merchant Taylor Hall in York.

SANDBURN

lodges, soon to be joined by an Equestrian Centre. All these businesses are now run by members of the Hogg family.

'The Dalesman' homes were later joined by the 'Deanery' collection with an elegant period look inspired by the Victorian era. Features included fireplaces built to an original Victorian design, picture and dado rails and 'egg and dart' plaster cornicing. In 1995 the 'Redmayne' development featuring the Deanery houses was built in Strensall and to add to the community a village hall and park were built in the village. Mallison Hill Easingwold, Kerver Lane, Dunnington and Vine Farm, Bubwith were similarly large developments that followed shortly afterwards. Mallison Hill was a fine example of a large scheme in a rural area backing onto the stunning Hambleton Hills. The development was built on the site of the old Claypenny hospital and made extensive use of existing mature landscaping, winning several design awards.

Elsewhere to the south building continued at Melbourne and Holme on Spalding Moor. In the east came new homes at Wetwang and East Cottingwith.

Above: Griffon Forest's luxury holiday lodges.
Below: Deanery Homes at Mallison Hill, Easingwold.

In 2001 the unearthing of an Iron Age grave by Hogg the Builder at one of its sites gave the firm national headlines again. The building firm was inundated with enquiries about its new development at Wetwang following the discovery of the skeleton of the Iron Age aristocrat and her chariot during excavations. The gravesite had lain undisturbed since the third or fourth century BC, some centuries before Queen Boadicea and her daughters made their famous, fatal and ultimately futile, attempt to expel the Romans from Britain. The grave was the oldest to contain a chariot ever found in Britain. The British Museum's curator for the Iron Age Dr Jeremy Hill described the finds, which became exhibits at his museum, as 'stunning'.

In 2001 the firm was building in the heart of York with developments of larger properties at Willow Grove Earswick and Farrier's Chase Strensall. They also carried out a number of unique barn conversions at Sycamore Farm Strensall.

Years on from the foresight of people working from home, there was now a requirement for office space at home. In the two years which followed the firm

Above: Excavating the Iron Age grave in Wetwang unearthed by Hogg the Builder. *Above inset, top right:* A reconstruction of the excavated chariot. *Below:* Hogg's vintage style bus. It was seen during the 1980's and 1990's at many events throughout the country including agricultural shows, sporting events and even weddings.

landscaped gardens, are all included in many of their homes. Whether clients are moving into one of Hogg's five bedroom detached homes or two bedroom terraced home, they will invariably be impressed with the design, quality and location of their new homes.

developed homes with work studios above garages for flexible living and working environments at sites including Derwent Chase at Barmby on the Marsh.

Building locally within the Vale of York Hogg the Builders' developments are small and select, attracting many repeat customers, who remain loyal to the Hogg brand. They are set in villages, or small country towns, and thoughtfully planned to fit in with their environment. Each home is designed to both suit its position and meet the wishes of the buyer therefore there are rarely two houses on a Hogg development which are quite the same. Here is a builder who will go a long way to meet clients' ideas about the kind of home they want and if a property is sold off-plan or at an early stage in the build process there is even greater flexibility. Each home features a unique Hogg brick which is hand crafted by Roy Mason who has worked with the company since 1978 and is now training his son to continue this great tradition.

At each of more than 30 stages in the construction of a house a close inspection is carried out by one of the site supervisors. Before any home is handed over it is personally checked by one of the New Homes managers. Every buyer is invited to join them on this tour of inspection and recent customer care surveys have revealed 100% customer satisfaction. Rooted in the Vale of York for 40 years, they have a unique understanding of the area, the people and their needs.

With Hogg the Builder, quality really does come as standard, right down to the fixtures and fittings – range cookers, integrated appliances, oak floors, digital surround sound, cctv and

What next for Hogg the Builder? Hogg aims to continue these traditions whilst meeting the needs of the 21st century customer. At the forefront of these plans is the scheme featuring seven hundred new homes at Germany Beck, Fulford and the company's first £1 million properties at Ilford Court, Earswick.

Top left: Increased house sizes and specification at Barmby on the Marsh. Top right: Local craftsman Roy Mason with a hand crafted Hogg Brick which can be found in every house built by Hogg the Builder. Below: The Riseborough at High Garth, Earswick internals; (inset) at the Sidings, Strensall.

Shouksmith - Working Together

Ever wondered where you might find craftsmen skilled enough to be entrusted with the challenging task of replacing the copper roof on York Minster? Look no further than Shouksmiths in Murton Way.

With bases in Leeds, Bolton, Sheffield and Gloucester as well as in York, today the Shouksmith group is a national presence. It is however through the original York-based arm of Shouksmiths that the group - J H Shouksmith & Sons Ltd - that the group can trace its beginnings.

In 1787 the marriage of Jonas Shouksmith of Bradford to Mary Plummer in Micklegate provided him not only with a wife but also a new home. He was a brewer by trade, an occupation which he followed for several years, living in Tanner Row. In 1806 he purchased his freemanship of the City of York, describing himself as an 'ale-draper' who was obviously selling his own brew.

Since then there have to date been six further generations of Shouksmith descendents working in York, each generation with its own representatives amongst Freemen of the City.

Jonas and Mary's second son, Joseph Richard Shouksmith, turned his back on brewing and was apprenticed to John Jackson, a plumber. He became a Master Craftsman but had to become a Freeman too before he was allowed to employ workmen. When he became a Freeman of the City in 1820 it was he who established the company which exists to this day.

By 1822 Joseph Richard Shouksmith was advertising in the City of York Directory, calling himself 'Plumber and Glazier' trading from St Mary's Row, Bishophill. Joseph had married his old master John Jackson's daughter, Hannah.

The Shouksmith family have a long connection with Micklegate, moving into number 59 (now number 128) Micklegate in 1824.

Joseph and Hannah's elder son, Thomas, would in turn join the business.

Thomas Shouksmith died in 1861 leaving six young children and a widow, Ann, who took responsibility for the business until her own death in 1864. Now in his old age Joseph Richard Shouksmith again briefly took up the reins until his death in 1866, when two of his grandsons, Joseph and John Henry, continued the business together until in 1878 the latter bought it giving it its long-lived name of JH Shouksmith. Meanwhile Thomas's other sons established their own businesses in Fairfax Street and Blossom Street, York.

John Henry Shouksmith married Julia Mary North in 1872. Her father was manager of the York Union Banking Company. They had

Top left: *Thomas Henry Shouksmith 1873 - 1969.* **Above:** *The beautiful, hand-painted certificate presented to Thomas Henry, on the occasion of 75 years with the company, by his co-directors and staff of the firm.* **Left:** *The rear of the Micklegate premises in 1902.*

five children, and their two sons, Thomas Henry and Arthur William, would in due turn grow up to work with their father.

In 1913, a year before the outbreak of the first world war, John Henry Shouksmith took the first of two radical steps in the company's history: firstly he entered into a formal deed of partnership with his two sons Thomas and Arthur. Secondly, in 1919, the partnership was ended, and instead Shouksmiths became a limited liability company, one of the first in York. When John Henry died in 1924, his elder son, Thomas, became Chairman, and with his brother Arthur now ran the company for many years.

In fact those 'many years' would be many decades. At the age of 90 Thomas was presented with a service certificate celebrating 75 years with the company.

Both Thomas and Arthur Shouksmith continued taking an active interest in the business until their deaths in 1969 and 1968 respectively: their service to the company had jointly amounted to an extraordinary 154 years.

Left: David Dutton and Charlie Mitchell relaying the lead on the roof of All Saints Church, Coppergate in 1944. Below: Below: An example of a classical lead rainwater head and pipe for restoration work in the 1950s.

Thomas had no children to follow him, but Arthur's elder son William Henry (known as Harry) Shouksmith became Chairman whilst his younger brother Philip Harold also joined the business.

William Henry Shouksmith had already been largely responsible for expanding the business in the era following the second world war when building was at its peak.

In 1987 following the death of William Henry his nephews Colin Maxwell Foster, and Richard Philip Shouksmith (Philip Harold's son), took over the running of the business, doing so until 2003.

The growth of the company since the end of the second world war has inevitably been affected by the ups and downs of the national economy, but it has always responded well to every challenge, growing into a group covering most of England. Down the decades it has successfully diversified into lead work, industrial heating and air conditioning, property owning and development in addition to the original plumbing work.

Shouksmiths would become a major specialist in lead, copper and stainless steel sheet roofing. For all these services it provides full design facilities as required.

The Shouksmith group would in due course have divisions not only in York but also in Leeds, Gloucester and Worksop. Turner & Pritchard Ltd in Gloucester joined the Group in 1966. This division has traded as Shouksmiths since May 2006. In 1976 H Morfitt & Son Ltd of Leeds too joined the Group, further, strengthening the commercial and industrial mechanical capability.

Further geographical expansion took place in 1985 when Briggs and Hunt in Worksop was acquired.

From Leeds it carried out industrial and commercial heating, ventilation and air conditioning throughout the UK. From the other premises it concentrates on plumbing work including drainage, rainwater systems, hot and cold services, sanitation and gas, all types of building and domestic heating including sheltered accommodation.

Increasingly the Heating and Ventilating division in Leeds was finding it necessary to form partnerships with electrical subcontractors to satisfy clients' work methods. In 1999, an electrical subcontracting company was acquired enabling the Leeds division to now offer the complete Building Services package.

At the beginning of 1996 the Group was restructured and the former subsidiary companies ceased to operate. Their trading activities were all transferred to trading divisions of J H Shouksmith & Sons Ltd, each now coming under the Shouksmiths name.

Top: Directors of the company in 1963, from left; brothers Arthur William Shouksmith and Thomas Henry Shouksmith and William Henry Shouksmith, son of Arthur William. Left: Phil Oates and apprentice Scott McCarthy prepare lead in front of Allerton Castle near Knaresborough.

Managing Director, Colin Foster, retired from the everyday running of the business but continue to manage the company's property portfolio.

Following that change John Miller who had joined the Leeds division's founding company in 1965 took over as Managing Director whist Mark Foster became company Finance Director.

Richard Shouksmith remains Chairman: his two sons David and Edward joined the business in 2005 and 2001. David as a project manager and Edward as an estimator.

All Richard Shouksmith's three children, Claire, David and Edward became Freemen of the City of York in 2006 continuing the tradition started by their Great-Great-Great-Great Grandfather.

Throughout its history, the company has done work on many notable buildings but none gave more pleasure than the contract to replace the copper roof on the North Transept to York Minster with lead in 1989. The company believes that the high reputation that it enjoys is confirmed by the majority of its work being repeat business. Its commitment to its staff is demonstrated by its having presented over 140 gold watches for long service. If Jonas Shouksmith could have seen into the future of the family he founded on his marriage to Mary Plummer more than 200 years ago, he would undoubtedly have been greatly surprised to see just how many of his descendants still live in York. Equally he would have been proud to know that the firm founded by his son, and now a diversified group of companies, still continues to offer traditional plumbing work to a standard of which he would have approved.

Meanwhile after several difficult trading years, in 2005 the Worksop division was moved to Sheffield with its much larger demand for services. The new arrangement was soon working successfully.

In 2006, a plumbing and domestic heating subcontractor in Bolton, the Keda Plumbing Company Ltd which now trades as Shouksmiths, was purchased, so opening up a new market in the North-West. The company is now actively looking for further geographical expansion.

Meanwhile in 2007 the Group's Leeds division moved its accommodation from the middle of Headingley to a purpose built office on the motorway system on the outskirts of Leeds.

Today the once-small family business is a substantial group with an annual turnover of more than £21 million. The Group now employs over 200 people processing full Mechanical, Electrical and Plumbing contracts up to an individual project value of £5m.

Though a limited company the Group remains a family enterprise, and is set to continue as such into the future.

In 2002, Colin Foster's son Mark joined the business. The following year the then Chairman, Richard Shouksmith and

*Top left: David, Claire and Edward become Freemen of the City of York in 2006. **Above left:** Chris White commissioning a boiler installation. **Below:** From left, Edward, David and Richard Shouksmith at The Plaza development in Leeds*

Askham Bryan College - Planting New Thoughts

Seeking an understanding of the land and its flora and fauna has been a fundamental part of the human experience since time immemorial. Today, passing on both traditional and innovative old knowledge whilst planting new thoughts in developing minds is something at which Askham Bryan College excels.

Askham Bryan College, situated on a ridge on the edge of the Vale of York, is located just four miles from York. The main campus of this 'land-based' college is one of the most attractive in the country. The extensive grounds include not only the College's farm and horticultural unit but also woodlands, a small lake and excellent outdoor sports facilities. As well as providing its students with a marvellous setting, it also offers excellent resources and facilities to help them with their studies.

Due to its long history and changing county boundaries today's Askham Bryan College has had a number of different names during its existence. The College evolved following a series of initiatives to develop formal agricultural and horticultural education in Yorkshire, and students both old and new still hotly debate even the date of its foundation.

Agricultural education in Yorkshire was first established under the direction of the Yorkshire Council for Agricultural Education as long ago as 1898. The Council consisted of representatives of the three Ridings of Yorkshire and Leeds University. At the outset a farm was leased at Garforth, though this was given up in 1927.

It was in 1927 that two farms, Westfield and East Barrow, were acquired in the village of Askham Bryan outside York: they were predominantly used as demonstration and research farms by the University. A third holding would be added in 1937.

The first substantial proposal for a purpose-built residential institute was drawn up in 1927 but was not implemented for a number of years. However, some early instructional courses did take place on the site, one of the first being a poultry course held in 1932.

The development of a national agricultural policy in the 1930s, combined with the success of short courses in agriculture being offered by the Young Framers, paved the way for agreement to help to develop the site into a residential College.

The original proposals, dating from June 1934, estimated costs of £16,932 for a dairy, £6,400 for the horticultural unit, and £65,050 for educational buildings and hostels designed to provide accommodation for up to 60 students: considerable sums in those days.

The main college building, still a familiar landmark today, dates from the 1930s. But the outbreak of the second world

Top left, left and above: 1950s view of the Main Cowshed (top left), the Carnation House (left) and the Workshop (above). Right: One of the Applied Science Laboratories in the 1960s.

war meant it would be some years before the new institute was able to accept its first full-time students. During the early war years it was used for training land girls - press reports from November 1939 record newly recruited land army girls making turnip 'pies' at what was then named the Yorkshire Agricultural Institute, Askham Bryan. Later in the war the site was requisitioned and used as the Northern Command HQ, during which time extensive air raid shelters were constructed under the College lawns. In the closing years of the war the Institute housed the National Institute of Agricultural Engineering before being de-requisitioned in 1947. Considerable refurbishment was needed before the Institute could accept its first students.

The official history of today's College begins in January 1948 when the first students enrolled on residential courses at the then Yorkshire Institute of Agriculture, Askham Bryan under its Principal JA Lindsay. During those early years only male students were accepted, and only agriculture and horticulture courses were available. Smart dress was expected at all times, with a collar and tie being required even when students were engaged on practical outdoor work.

In 1954 the Yorkshire Council for Agricultural Education

ceased to exist. The running of the Institute was taken over solely by the West Riding of Yorkshire and became the Yorkshire (West Riding) Institute of Agriculture. By 1955, now under a new Principal KN Russell, there were 75 students at the College.

Lance Gilling became Principal in 1957; he would remain at the College for the next 27 years until his retirement in 1984.

In the 1960s, under Lance Gilling, came further development of the site with the building of the Conference Hall, new residential hostels, a teaching block and lecture theatre. The first female students, two ladies studying horticulture, enrolled in 1964. By 1968 the College had 150 students - and accommodation available for 50 more - and was renamed the Askham Bryan College of Agriculture and Horticulture.

By now the original three farms were divided into two main areas of activity: a farm of 440 acres, together with 65 acres concerned with horticultural production.

About 220 acres was grassland, whilst the remainder of the farmland was used to grow 40-50 acres of potatoes and around 30 acres of sugar beet, with the balance in wheat and barley. A 300-foot deep borehole supplied irrigation.

Dairy cows and pigs were the main livestock, with the 150-cow British Friesian and Ayrshire herd being milked in a new 8/16 'herringbone' milking parlour.

Top: Askham Bryan College group photograph, 1961.
Right: One of the Student Hostels and Student Study Bedroom (inset) of the late 1960s.

Some 120 Large White and Landacre sows, housed in modern buildings, were kept and fattened for bacon. Around 200 breeding sheep were also reared.

Elsewhere 6,000 poultry were kept, housed in deep litter systems or batteries, for egg production.

The main feature of the 65 acres devoted to horticulture was the 1.5 acres of heated glass, much of which had recently been rebuilt. Within the glasshouses were ornamental plants growing in different temperature regimes, propagation, and crops such as tomatoes, lettuces, carnations, chrysanthemums and pot plants. The heating system was both oil and coke-fired.

In addition a comprehensive range of herbaceous plants and shrubs were provided for teaching purposes. A limited area was devoted to top and soft fruit production and market crops.

Planting of trees had already been extensive. In particular two shelter belts of an interesting variety of trees, one on either side of the main building, had been established with the advice of the Forestry Commission, and were also used for teaching.

The year 1974 saw the first royal visit to the College, by the Duchess of Kent. Local government reorganisation and boundary changes that same year saw the College 'move' into North Yorkshire: due to more recent boundary changes the College is now within the City of York.

From 1948 to 1964 the only qualifications offered by the College had been National Certificates in Agriculture or Horticulture. During the 1970s however, the College began to offer a wider range of land-based subjects and a wider range of further education qualifications. Higher Education qualifications such as Higher National Diplomas were also introduced, and these were to be followed by Honours Degrees.

Today the College has over 650 full-time students, and more than 2,000 others who study on a part-time basis at the York campus and at the College's other centres throughout the region. Locations include Bedale, Guisborough, Harrogate, Pickering, Thirsk, Wakefield, Scarborough and Middlesbrough.

Students range from 16 to well over 65 years of age, and study for a number of different qualifications covering a wide range of topics. Subjects now include: agriculture; animal management; business & IT; countryside & environment; engineering & plant; equine; floristry; food; forestry & arboriculture; sports & green-keeping; horticulture; landscaping; land management, and travel & tourism.

With over £5 million of investment in recent years students and staff from the early years would notice many changes, but they would also find much that is familiar. Westfield, the original farm from pre-College days, still operates as a working farm but now boasts a robotic milking parlour, the Centre of Vocational Excellence in Food Chain Technology, and the National Beef Training Centre. The original dairy building is now a Learning Resource Centre including an extensive library and several IT suites. East Barrow has been converted into a Centre for Animal Management and houses the College's collection of exotic animals and the Veterinary Nursing Unit. The original horticultural glasshouses have been replaced by modern units. A new Equestrian Centre was opened in 2005, when horses once again joined the residential population at the College: the last farm horse having been previously sold in 1960.

Students with nostalgic memories of the residential accommodation built in the 1960s however will be disappointed. These 'period pieces' have now been demolished and replaced by plush en-suite accommodation with internet facilities – a far cry from the Spartan study/bedrooms of the 1940s and 1950s.

Top left: A view of one of the Agricultural Engineering Workshops, 1968. *Below:* Sheep shearing in progress in 1968. *Bottom:* Askham Bryan College, 2007.

Pilcher Developments
Homes for All, Yesterday and Today

Pilcher Developments is a well-established property developer which has an enviable reputation established over the firm's long history. Today the firm which came into being in 1964 is based at Tower House Askham Fields Lane in Askham Bryan near York.

The company now operates in three divisions. Pilcher Homes, Milton Westfield Ltd the Industrial arm of the business, and the commercial property division Pilcher Developments London Ltd.

Though Pilcher Developments Ltd may have only existed since 1964 its roots go much further back in time. The family firm in fact started building houses in Kent as long ago as 1897.

It was not until 1947 that the Pilcher family moved to Yorkshire and their firm began its rise to first local, and then national, prominence. Pilcher Homes began its first local development in 1956 at Acomb.

In the early 1960s however, predicting Pilcher's future would have been a hazardous undertaking: its office was nothing more than a 10 foot by 8 foot garden shed.

The company's second office was built on site at The Courtneys, Selby. When the firm moved from one building site to another the office went with it.

Following the second world war and the baby boom of the 1960s major house-building programmes led housing completions nationally to increase from just over 50,000 per annum to a peak of over 400,000 a year in 1968/9.

What seems remarkable today is just how little houses cost in the mid 1960s. A price list for over 40 houses under construction by Pilcher & Son in 1964 shows the most expensive as just £3,614 whilst the cheapest was a mere £2,050. Today houses costing up to three quarters of a million pounds are not uncommon!

But whether cheap or expensive the demand for housing would be maintained down the decades, with thousands of folk, both in and around York and further afield, eager to buy new houses built by Pilcher's.

Above: *An R D Pilcher & Son Ltd letterhead from 1965.*
Below: *A 1960s Pilcher housing estate development at Dunnington.*

council estate. Elsewhere in York the firm built Langley House the first development of sheltered homes to be offered for sale in the York area, providing a new level of security whilst enabling the owners to continue to enjoy a life of independence. Langley House would be made up of 68 luxury flats together with a comprehensive range of communal facilities and the services of a resident warden.

Today Pilcher Homes caters for the modern lifestyles of the 21st Century, with each of its new houses now offered with an integrated technology system – a far cry from those long ago days when a house could be bought for £2,000!

A fixed office was eventually found above a cycle shop at Gowthorpe near Selby. The expansion of the company however soon prompted the purchase of the Flaxley Road Laundry in Selby. This involved converting the laundry into a joiner's shop, and the laundry manager's house into Pilcher's new office.

In the 1980s it was decided to move the company offices to York. New offices at Barton House North Moor Road, Huntington were occupied in December 1987.

Top left: Bishopthorpe Garth, converted from a large private house into prestigious offices and new headquarters for the Pilcher Group in 1990. **Centre:** *Langley House sheltered homes.* **Below:** *Percy Pilcher (centre), Robert Pilcher (centre right) and John Penrose (right) at the topping out ceremony of Langley House.*

Staff would have only three years to get used to the new offices however before another move to even larger offices became necessary.

The conversion of an impressive private house, Bishopthorpe Garth, would supply what had by now become the Pilcher Group with a suite of prestigious offices set in its own grounds with attractive lawns, gardens and woodland. Visitors to the offices were occasionally surprised by the sound of gunshots as Managing Director and self-appointed gamekeeper Robert Pilcher attempted to keep down the local rabbit population from his office window overlooking the lawn!

In the meantime houses were not the only type of property being constructed by the firm. York's Albion Wharf in Skeldergate was one of Pilcher's many major projects. The 31,000 sq ft office block would occupy a riverside site in the very heart of York and be completed in 1990.

Sheltered housing too has been a specialty of Pilcher's locally and nationally. The company decided to enter the market for retirement homes in 1982. Notable projects have included work on a sheltered housing scheme for York City Council at Challoners Road in the middle of an existing

Monk Bridge Construction
The Champions of Steel

For two thousand years the City of York has been at the forefront of innovative construction techniques. From the Romans to the Normans and beyond York has always embraced the best of the times and incorporated the new with the old. Stone replaced wood. Today steel has staked a claim.

One of the best-known names in York is that of The Monk Bridge Construction Company Ltd. The firm of steel structural engineers is based on the Elvington Industrial Estate but for many decades it operated within the city from a site on the banks of the River Foss.

The business was founded on 13th June 1922 by Frederick Smith Fletcher, Samuel Edwin Fletcher, Samuel Henry Fletcher and Thompson Clegg.

At the outset the firm was based on land rented on Fossbank in York from the City Council.

Thomas Clegg took over sole ownership in December 1926. He was joined in 1931 by Mr AL Wrigley who later took over the company.

Above: Foss Bank Bridge built in 1933 and still standing toay. Right: Construction of the National Glass Company's York plant in the 1930s.

One of the most long lasting structures installed by the company would prove to be the Foss Ban Bridge, built in 1931 and still standing today.

During the war years York suffered extensive bomb damage. In late 1942 two gasholders near the company were destroyed. In the spirit of the times however, the proprietor laconically reported at the next Annual General Meeting 'It was gratifying to note that output had not been seriously upset owing to damage from the bomb blast on 17th December 1942'.

In October 1947 AL Wrigley sold the company to Harold Newsome and Mrs Bessie Emmett.

Part of the old gas works yard (now Sainsbury's) was bought in 1965 - the other part was owned by Bradley of York. A new works was now built when Geoffrey Newsome took over from his father Harold Newsome, whilst Peter Newsome took over an associated company, Harold Newsome Ltd in Leeds.

In 1968 the company was sold to Bradley of York, but subsequently went into receivership before being taken over by Dalehome Holdings from Lancashire and subsequently by Northern Developments.

In 1975 Geoffrey and Peter Newsome, together with their two sons, respectively Richard and Paul Newsome, bought back the two companies, Harold Newsome Ltd in Leeds and The Monk Bridge Construction Co Ltd of York. Not owning the land in York however, the Newsomes now bought a site at Elvington which they redeveloped.

Geoffrey and Richard Newsome ran the company from Elvington where they were joined by Tim Newsome. Geoffrey retired in 1985. Richard's sons Jonathan and Andrew have subsequently joined the family business.

Today the company is able to offer an impressive range of services to clients, either 'design and build' or building to a client's own designs.

In recent years contracts have included work on York's McArthur Glen Designer Outlet Village. Shepherd Construction Ltd won the main contract on a design and build basis, but went back to back with Monk Bridge Construction which re-designed the steelwork in conjunction with Shepherd Construction's architects and engineers forming 115 new shopping outlets and an eating area. The central core of the building project incorporated 25 metre long cambered steel beams.

That same year the company also worked with Henry Boot Construction Ltd to build Harrogate's new Hydro Pool, erecting curved tubular trusses over an existing excavation for the swimming pool. The trusses were delivered to the site in two and three pieces and then welded together. A 500 tonne crane lifted the trusses into position

Projects are endless, from the steel frame of a new Visitors' Centre at Tetley' Brewery in Leeds to the Ray Chapman Volvo dealership in Malton.

Perhaps one of the most challenging projects in recent years however was the erection of a spectacular curved roof at Stockton Riverside College. The project presented a unique challenge both because of the roof's unusual curved shape - each rafter with a different radius and each supporting steel 'tree' a different height - and because the pre-fabricated structure had to be installed by being lifted over the top of existing buildings.

But, no matter what the difficulties, since 1922 The Monk Bridge Construction Company's staff have always proved themselves more than equal to any challenge.

Top left: *Construction of the McArthur Glen Designer Outlet Village, York, 1998.* **Centre:** *Constructing the steel frame of a new Visitors' Centre at Tetley' Brewery in Leeds.* **Below:** *A view of the 'tree' suporting structures used in constructing the curved roof of the Stockton Riversde College.*

Turnbulls of York
Looking After The Discerning Motorist For Over Half A Century

Turnbulls, the successful Mazda dealership located along Layerthorpe Road in York can be proud of over half a century in business. The company was established in March 1952 by Robert Turnbull.

The founder was no stranger to enterprise and had already experienced success in the motor industry. From a very modest start Robert Turnbull built up his capital with a car repair business in his home town of Harrogate.

Close attention to the needs of his customers, and a natural gift with all things mechanical resulted in the growth of the business and this enabled Robert to extend the scope of his activities into petrol retailing.

Robert Turnbull
Founded the business in the early 1950s

|

Peter Turnbull
joined his father in 1958

|

Martyn Turnbull
and his brother
Paul Turnbull
joined their father in the mid 1980s

The early days in York
After a long search for a suitable location the site of a run-down filling station and garage in York was identified and acquired. Much modernisation was required - old-fashioned petrol pumps which swung across the pavement were still in use when Robert Turnbull took over! With remarkable self-belief and faith in his own ability, Robert set about the task of modernising and rebuilding the site to meet the needs of the increasingly discerning 1950s motorist.

Servicing cars and selling petrol from Holgate Bridge Filling Station continued for a decade until the business was sold in 1962. During the following five years Robert operated from a busy petrol station located at Monkbridge, York,

selling Cleveland fuel. The Cleveland organisation was later bought out by the mighty 'Esso' corporation.

Peter Turnbull, Robert's son, had joined his father in the family business in 1958 and began selling cars to a growing band of eager customers by 1961.

The move to Layerthorpe Road
Next came the move to the present site, 17-27 Layerthorpe Road, in 1967 and a change in the trading name to 'R & P Turnbull' reflecting Peter Turnbull's increasing contribution to the running of the business.

Expansion characterised the following years and the development of the business. A crucial milestone in the history of the company was passed when it secured the franchise for Mazda cars. Mazda U.K. Ltd. are known to be very demanding of the individual dealers which make up their network, and Turnbulls appointment in the York area was one of their proudest moments.

One of the signs of a successful business is undoubtedly the level of repeat business it manages to achieve. This is yet another source of pride at Turnbulls of York as they have individual customers who have been supplied with cars by them for over 30 years. Most of these highly satisfied customers are private individuals and the principals of many of the small businesses which thrive in York and the surrounding district. There are exceptions to this - and a significant proportion of the business is secured from other parts of the U.K. - and the occasional export order, including one from Pakistan!

Further expansion
It has been a challenge for the premises at Layerthorpe Road to cope with the expansion of the business over the years. Land has been acquired at the side and rear of the original site to allow

for the growth and a superbly equipped workshop complete with state-of-the-art technology sits at the hub of the Turnbull Mazda operation. An ever growing band of delighted customers is assured by the after-sales expertise of Martyn and Paul Turnbull, grandsons of the founder, who have been involved in the business since the mid-1980s.

The motor trade is more competitive than ever at the dawn of a new millennium, and many of the smaller independent motor dealerships have been swallowed up by the more impersonal national chains.

Personal service and quality cars
Personal service and attention to detail are just two of the formidable weapons in the Turnbull armoury. These, combined with the quality and renowned reliability of the Mazda cars which are sold by the company will ensure that Turnbulls Mazda will continue to look after the interests of its customers well into the new century. A point illustrated by one valued client who visited the dealership after a long absence and explained:

"I have kept my present car far too long because it has been so reliable."

Left, above and below: Turnbulls state-of-the-art premises on Layerthorpe Road.

Ingleby's Coaches - Travelling in Style

Ingleby's Coaches Ltd based in Hospital Fields Road is York's oldest continually family-operated coach company in the city.

The coaching trade in York has an ancient pedigree. Before the coming of the railways in the 19th century horse drawn coaches and coaching inns were a common sight in the City. But York's association with coaches goes back much further. To the very first coaches ever seen in England in fact.

When Richard II visited York during his turbulent reign in the 14th century he did so riding in something quite new - a coach.

Coaches are named after a small Hungarian village, Kocs, where superior wagons, carts and carriages were built. Kocs, in the

Hungarian district of Komarom-Esztergom, lies on the main road along the Danube between Vienna and Budapest. These two great cities needed well-built, fast vehicles that would carry more than two people over the bumpy roads of the day in as much comfort as possible.

In Hungarian one of the best of these multi-horse carts was called kocsi szekér 'a wagon from Kocs.' In Kocs, one of the first successful, reasonably comfortable passenger coaches, a light, graceful, four-wheeled wagon with a strap suspension was built. Its design was so compact, elegant and sturdy that this coach design spread throughout Europe in the 15th and 16th centuries.

The German-speaking Viennese started to call this vehicle a Kutsche, which is the way heard Hungarians pronouncing the name of the little carriage-making town. From Vienna these lively vehicles travelled to Paris and the French, adapting the Austrian word, called it a coche. In Rome it was, and

Above: Founder Christopher Ingleby. Right: The company's first coach, a twelve seater Ford Transit Mini Bus, 1968. Below: Ingleby's second Mini Bus acquired in 1972.

Increasing business brought with it the opportunity for expansion. In 1986 Ingleby's took over competitors Bailey's Coach Company in Fangfoss, though it was not for some years later that this operation would be brought under the Ingleby's name.

Today the company now operates 12 coaches varying in size from 12 to 53 seaters, the majority of which are manufactured by Volvo and Mercedes.

Many customers return time and time again: the firm is particularly proud that one of Christopher Ingleby's very first clients still uses the company today, four decades after the first contract.

still is, in Italian cocchio. Eventually the English borrowed the word and the vehicle and called it a coach.

When Anne of Bohemia married England's Richard II in 1382 she brought carriages from Kocs, Hungary with her to England, ensuring that she and the King could travel in relative comfort around their realm.

Ingleby's Coaches Ltd may not be able to claim to trace its roots back to the 14th Century, but it can rightly claim that its coaches are undoubtedly even more comfortable than those used by Richard II and his Queen.

The firm was founded in May 1968 by Christopher Ingleby. At the outset he operated just one single 12-seater Ford Transit mini-bus from his home, trading under the name of Ingleby's Mini Coaches.

Between 1970 and 1971 two more 12-seater mini-busses were acquired.

The first move up to larger coaches came in 1972 when Christopher bought a 29-seater Bedford, an acquisition which made it necessary to also find a larger base of operations. As a consequence a move was made to rented premises on Rufforth Airfield to the west of York, premises which would be occupied for the following five years. In celebration of the new purchase the trading name was changed to Ingleby's Luxury Coaches.

In 1977 new premises were bought on the Fulford Industrial estate, premises which are still the company's base today, incorporating its workshops and offices. The following year the business became a limited company.

Clients range from private individuals, various local and national organisations, schools, universities and Government bodies. Foreign clients include groups from North America, Europe and Australia, many of over 30 years standing, some of whom have become firm friends.

As for the standard of luxury now offered, Richard II and Queen Anne would have considered today's coaches nothing short of magical. Reclining seats, videos, matched by with unprecedented comfort and reliability, all combining to ensure that the Ingleby's name can stake its own claim to a place in York's history.

Above: A 1963 Plaxton Panama body on a Leyland Leopard chassis. This 49 seater was owned by Ingleby's from 1974, and is now in preservation at the Ribble Preservation Society. Below: One of Ingleby's fleet of 2007.

William Birch - Building A Name

York has been notable for its building work since Roman times. Today one of the most prestigious names amongst Britain's building contractors is the award-winning York-based firm of William Birch & Sons Ltd founded in the 1870s.

With headquarters in Link Road Court, Osbaldwick, York, and with a new office in Leeds, William Birch & Sons Ltd's team of over 100 employees deals with a wide variety of projects throughout Yorkshire, ranging from local maintenance works to contracts worth several million for major regional clients, in the public, private and heritage sectors.

Turnover has increased from £7 million to over £20 million over the past few years, enhanced by the opening of a Leeds office and a new Hire Centre in York.

The firm's services include new-build construction, civil engineering, restoration and refurbishment, equipment and lorry hire together with commercial and industrial development.

William Birch established the firm in York in 1874 in partnership with a Mr G Naylor. The firm erected both the York Public Library and the Friends Meeting Room in Clifford Street, Groves Wesleyan Chapel and the Soldiers Home in Wenlock Terrace. The partnership ended in 1889 though by then William had been joined in the business by his three sons.

The eldest son, William Henry Birch, Lord Mayor and Alderman of York, took over in 1913 on his father's death: he had left school at the age of 12 in 1883 and began his working life wheeling tarmacadam for resurfacing Ambrose Street- a task so tough that he later attributed his slightly bowed leg to the job.

The business, now a limited company, developed and expanded throughout the first world war and beyond.

In 1913 the firm had a horse and tipping cart, and a flat wagon. Any other transport horse carts and handcarts – the latter used mainly for jobbing work – were hired. By the 1920s the firm not only had its horse and cart but had also acquired a three-ton Daimler flat wagon, a Model T three-way tipping lorry and an ex-army Commer – though this last seldom ran.

board appointees Paul Goyea as Construction Director and Alistair Birch, the fifth generation of the Birch family, as Company Secretary.

During the 1920s the family's third generation in the business, Arnold and Jack Birch joined the company, having both served craft apprenticeships. By then the firm was building part of the post-war new housing in Tang Hall estate. Such post-war reconstruction work in York consolidated the success and reputation of the company which saw considerable expansion.

In the 1960s John Birch the next generation of the Birch family joined the company with a degree in construction and experience with national contractors. Also during the 1960s the company passed the £1million annual turnover for the first time.

Christopher Birch, also a fourth generation family member, joined the company in the 1970s with a degree in Civil Engineering and experience with national contractors.

In the next decade the company built itself new premises in York City centre to cope with continued expansion. By the time the company celebrated is 125th Anniversary in the 1990s annual turnover had reached £7million.

By 2001 when a small works office was established in Horsforth, Leeds, the company turnover has grown to over £16 million.

The following year the company constructed and moved into new offices adjoining its plant hire operation on a site close to the A64 bypass at Osbaldwick.

Managing Director John Birch retired in 2002. Chairman Jack Birch died in 2003 whilst long-serving director David Field retired in 2006 and Company Secretary Tony Wright in 2007.

Chris Birch is now Chairman and Managing Director. He and David Holden Commercial Director have been joined by new

More speculative development work is now being undertaken, enhancing the flow of construction work, bringing annual turnover to £25 million - a fourfold increase in a decade. Recent prestigious contracts include an award-winning restoration of the long-abandoned Gibson Mill in Hebden Bridge for the National Trust.

With individual contract sizes moving up to £4 million for the first time on the restoration of Shibden Park in Halifax and the construction of a new monastery at Wass on the edge of the North Yorkshire moors, and several other important development projects in the pipeline the future looks even brighter than the past for William Birch & Sons.

*Top, facing page: First and second generation, founder William Birch (left) and his son William Henry Birch. **Facing page left, far left and this page:** Historical and recent projects of William Birch & Son Ltd: York Power Station Cooling Tower, Foss Islands, 1942 (far left, facing page), the Abbey Church Ampleforth College, 1958 (left, facing page), West Riding of Yorkshire Police Hostel, Wakefield, 1965 (top left), William Birch & Sons offices, Link Road Court, Osbaldwick (below) and the Urology Department of St James Hospital, Leeds, 2003 (above right).*

William Anelay Ltd

A Forward Thinking Approach To Preserving The Past

Founded in 1747 William Anelay Ltd is amongst the United Kingdom's leading and longest-established specialists in building conservation and restoration. Based in Osbaldwick, York, the firm has worked on many fine historic buildings and monuments throughout the British Isles and overseas as far away as Japan.

The business was founded by John Thompson (1714-1771), who was a Doncaster bricklayer and builder. John Thompson's daughter married into the Anelay family in 1740, but within a year her husband had died. Her husband's brother, Thomas Anelay, was also in the building trade and so John Thompson invited him to join his business in 1767 and become his successor.

From the outset the firm specialised mainly in brickwork and contributing to local buildings such as the Mansion House, the Rossington Rectory and the Judges and Stewards Stand at the Racecourse. The company's core business in restoration and conservation would begin when it was approached to carry out renovations on properties that it had originally built.

By the 1850s the firm was producing stone masonry works in a serious way, so beginning its long association with ecclesiastical and heritage properties. In the early 1900s the firm relocated to York, although the Anelay family name first appears in York records as far back as the 16th century.

The opening of premises in York was in part due to the friendship between Walter H Brierley (partner in an architectural firm founded by John Carr) and Thomas Anelay. They had collaborated on buildings in West Yorkshire and Brierley encouraged the firm to come to York and take advantage of building opportunities there. Thomas Anelay was responsible for the Company during and after World War I - his bearded, pipe-smoking features are wittily immortalised by York carver Wilfrid Milburn in the pediment above Thomas' Hotel on Museum Street.

The company now provides employment for 120 people, with a core of highly skilled trades including stonemasons, bricklayers, lead workers and joiners. Anelays offers a number of apprenticeship programmes to ensure that specialist craft skills are not lost. Employees take great pride in their acquired skills,

Above: *Thomas Anelay VI's bearded, pipe-smoking features wittily immortalised by York carver Wilfrid Milburn in the pediment above Thomas' Hotel on Museum Street.*
Below left: *Architect Walter H Brierley's house, Bishopsbarns, one of the company's many projects.*
Below: *Thorpe Underwood Hall (now Queen Ethelburga's School) re-built in Tudor style after a fire in 1895.*

with the firm having a remarkably high retention rate in comparison with its competitors. Master Stonemason Lyn Letby for example was with company for almost 50 years until retiring in 2006. Fellow stonemason Alan Abbott is still with the company after joining as a 16-year-old apprentice in 1963.

Amongst the firm's many prestigious 20th century projects in and around York have been a new wing at the Grade I listed King's Manor School; Architect Walter H Brierley's own house, Bishopsbarns, in St. Georges Place; Goddards in Tadcaster Road, originally built for chocolate manufacturer Noel Goddard Terry and now owned by the National Trust; Thorpe Underwood Hall (now Queen Ethelburga's School) – rebuilt after a fire in 1895 in Tudor style, using as much salvaged material as possible from the original building; and the restorations of Middlethorpe Hall and Nunnington Hall.

Due to the demands for the company's specialist skills, a second office has been opened in Manchester to support high profile projects in the North West such as Gorton Monastery and the Victoria Baths (winner of the BBC's first Restoration programme).

In January 2006 the company was acquired by its management team with Charles Anelay (the eighth generation of his family in the business) still taking a very active role as Special Projects Director.

Despite fierce competition down the years Anelays celebrates its 260th anniversary in 2007. It has survived and prospered by combining long-standing traditional building expertise and centuries-old craftsmanship with the best of modern-management. As a result Anelays has won a number of awards in recognition of its contribution to conservation and restoration.

Whilst working closely with architects and conservation groups such as English Heritage and the National Trust, Anelays continues to look for new business opportunities. In recent years the company has extended its expertise and its knowledge of its markets to meet the needs of those private householders who want their homes sympathetically restoring or extending in keeping with their original design and environment.

In an age where recycling and sustainability of natural resources have become major issues, the demand for conservation and

restoration is ever increasing. William Anelay Ltd aims to build long lasting business relationships, and work in partnership to exceed its clients' expectations.

Top left: A company photograph from 1972 with a young Charles Anelay. *Left:* Employee Alan Abbott at work. *Below:* The William Anelay Team 2007.

BIRDS EYE VIEW

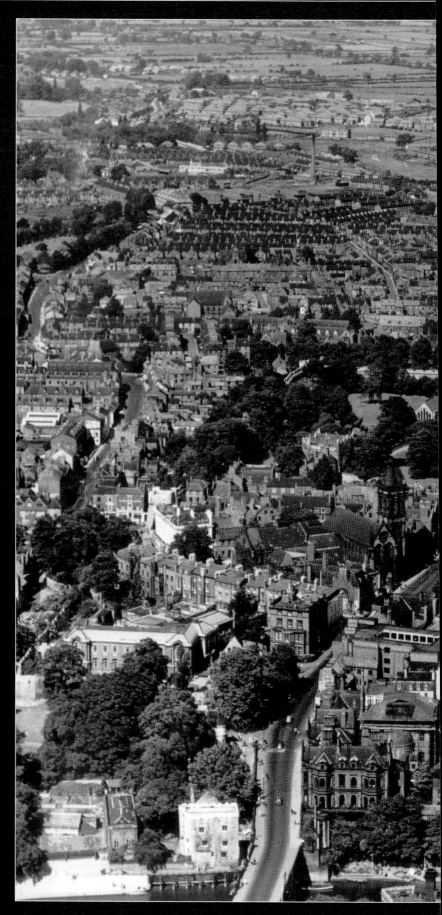

A delightful view of the centre of York which dates from May 1959. Many changes have taken place to the city in the 40 years or so since that time. The gentle curve of the River Ouse dominates the lower half of the picture and two of York's bridges, the Lendal (on the left) and the Ouse (on the right) are clearly in view. Rougier Street and North Street can be seen on the right of the photograph along with the historic buildings just a short distance across the water between Coney Street and the Ouse. As a point of reference, the roof of the Minster can be seen half way up the picture on the left. The bottom left hand corner of the photograph shows the Museum Gardens - the grounds where once stood St, Mary's Benedictine Abbey. This is, of course, the location of the world-famous York Mystery Plays.

A delightful view of the centre of York which dates from 1959. Many changes have taken place in the city in the 40 years or so since that time. The gentle curve of the River Ouse dominates the lower half of the picture and two of York's bridges, the Lendal (on the left) and the Ouse (on the right) are clearly in view. Rougier Street and North Street can be seen on the right of the photograph along with the historic building just a short distance across the water between Coney Street and the Ouse. As a point of reference , the roof of the Minster can be seen towards the top left of the picture. The bottom left hand corner of the photograph shows the Museum Gardens - the grounds where once stood St Mary's Benedictine Abbey.

ACKNOWLEDGMENTS

The publishers would like to thank

Local Studies Department, City of York Libraries
Ryedale Folk Museum
The Northern Echo, Newsquest North East Limited

Andrew Mitchell

Steve Ainsworth

Seamus Molloy

True North Books Ltd - Book List

Memories of Accrington - 1 903204 05 4

Memories of Barnet - 1 903204 16 X

Memories of Barnsley - 1 900463 11 3

More Memories of Barnsley - 1 903 204 79 8

Golden Years of Barnsley -1 900463 87 3

Memories of Basingstoke - 1 903204 26 7

Memories of Bedford - 1 900463 83 0

More Memories of Bedford - 1 903204 33 X

Golden Years of Birmingham - 1 900463 04 0

Birmingham Memories - 1 903204 45 3

More Birmingham Memories - 1 903204 80 1

Memories of Blackburn - 1 900463 40 7

More Memories of Blackburn - 1 900463 96 2

Memories of Blackpool - 1 900463 21 0

Memories of Bolton - 1 900463 45 8

More Memories of Bolton - 1 900463 13 X

Bolton Memories - 1 903204 37 2

Memories of Bournemouth -1 900463 44 X

Memories of Bradford - 1 900463 00 8

More Memories of Bradford - 1 900463 16 4

More Memories of Bradford II - 1 900463 63 6

Bradford Memories - 1 903204 47 X

More Bradford Memories - 1 903204 92 5

Bradford City Memories - 1 900463 57 1

Memories of Bristol - 1 900463 78 4

More Memories of Bristol - 1 903204 43 7

Memories of Bromley - 1 903204 21 6

Memories of Burnley - 1 900463 95 4

Golden Years of Burnley - 1 900463 67 9

Memories of Bury - 1 900463 90 3

More Memories of Bury - 1 903 204 78 X

Memories of Cambridge - 1 900463 88 1

Memories of Cardiff - 1 900463 14 8

More Memories of Cardiff - 1 903204 73 9

Memories of Carlisle - 1 900463 38 5

Memories of Chelmsford - 1 903204 29 1

Memories of Cheltenham - 1 903204 17 8

Memories of Chester - 1 900463 46 6

More Memories of Chester -1 903204 02 X

Chester Memories - 1 903204 83 6

Memories of Chesterfield -1 900463 61 X

More Memories of Chesterfield - 1 903204 28 3

Memories of Colchester - 1 900463 74 1

Nostalgic Coventry - 1 900463 58 X

Coventry Memories - 1 903204 38 0

Memories of Croydon - 1 900463 19 9

More Memories of Croydon - 1 903204 35 6

Golden Years of Darlington - 1 900463 72 5

Nostalgic Darlington - 1 900463 31 8

Darlington Memories - 1 903204 46 1

Memories of Derby - 1 900463 37 7

More Memories of Derby - 1 903204 20 8

Memories of Dewsbury & Batley - 1 900463 80 6

Memories of Doncaster - 1 900463 36 9

More Memories of Doncaster - 1 903204 75 5

Nostalgic Dudley - 1 900463 03 2

Golden Years of Dudley - 1 903204 60 7

Memories of Edinburgh - 1 900463 33 4

More memories of Edinburgh - 1903204 72 0

Memories of Enfield - 1 903204 14 3

Memories of Exeter - 1 900463 94 6

Memories of Glasgow - 1 900463 68 7

More Memories of Glasgow - 1 903204 44 5

Memories of Gloucester - 1 903204 04 6

Memories of Grimsby - 1 900463 97 0

More Memories of Grimsby - 1 903204 36 4

Memories of Guildford - 1 903204 22 4

Memories of Halifax - 1 900463 05 9

More Memories of Halifax - 1 900463 06 7

Golden Years of Halifax - 1 900463 62 8

Nostalgic Halifax - 1 903204 30 5

Memories of Harrogate - 1 903204 01 1

Memories of Hartlepool - 1 900463 42 3

Memories of High Wycombe - 1 900463 84 9

Memories of Huddersfield - 1 900463 15 6

More Memories of Huddersfield - 1 900463 26 1

Golden Years of Huddersfield - 1 900463 77 6

Nostalgic Huddersfield - 1 903204 19 4

Huddersfield Memories - 1903204 86 0

Huddersfield Town FC - 1 900463 51 2

Memories of Hull - 1 900463 86 5

More Memories of Hull - 1 903204 06 2

Hull Memories - 1 903204 70 4

Memories of Keighley - 1 900463 01 6

True North Books Ltd - Book List

Golden Years of Keighley - 1 900463 92 X
Memories of Kingston - 1 903204 24 0
Memories of Leeds - 1 900463 75 X
More Memories of Leeds - 1 900463 12 1
Golden Years of Leeds - 1 903204 07 0
Leeds Memories - 1 903204 62 3
More Leeds Memories - 1 903204 90 9
Memories of Leicester - 1 900463 08 3
More Memories of Leicester - 1 903204 08 9
Memories of Leigh - 1 903204 27 5
Memories of Lincoln - 1 900463 43 1
Memories of Liverpool - 1 900463 07 5
More Memories of Liverpool - 1 903204 09 7
Liverpool Memories - 1 903204 53 4
More Liverpool Memories - 1 903204 88 7
Memories of Luton - 1 900463 93 8
Memories of Macclesfield - 1 900463 28 8
Memories of Manchester - 1 900463 27 X
More Memories of Manchester - 1 903204 03 8
Manchester Memories - 1 903204 54 2
More Manchester Memories - 1 903204 89 5
Memories of Middlesbrough - 1 900463 56 3
More Memories of Middlesbrough - 1 903204 42 9
Memories of Newbury - 1 900463 79 2
Memories of Newcastle - 1 900463 81 4
More Memories of Newcastle - 1 903204 10 0
Newcastle Memories - 1.903204 71 2
Memories of Newport - 1 900463 59 8
Memories of Northampton - 1 900463 48 2
More Memories of Northampton - 1 903204 34 8
Memories of Norwich - 1 900463 73 3
Memories of Nottingham - 1 900463 91 1
More Memories of Nottingham - 1 903204 11 9
Nottingham Memories - 1 903204 63 1
Bygone Oldham - 1 900463 25 3
Memories of Oldham - 1 900463 76 8
More Memories of Oldham - 1 903204 84 4
Memories of Oxford - 1 900463 54 7
Memories of Peterborough - 1 900463 98 9
Golden Years of Poole - 1 900463 69 5
Memories of Portsmouth - 1 900463 39 3
More Memories of Portsmouth - 1 903204 51 8
Nostalgic Preston - 1 900463 50 4
More Memories of Preston - 1 900463 17 2
Preston Memories - 1 903204 41 0
Memories of Reading - 1 900463 49 0
Memories of Rochdale - 1 900463 60 1

More Memories of Reading - 1 903204 39 9
More Memories of Rochdale - 1 900463 22 9
Memories of Romford - 1 903204 40 2
Memories of Rothertham- 1903204 77 1
Memories of St Albans - 1 903204 23 2
Memories of St Helens - 1 900463 52 0
Memories of Sheffield - 1 900463 20 2
More Memories of Sheffield - 1 900463 32 6
Golden Years of Sheffield - 1 903204 13 5
Sheffield Memories - 1 903204 61 5
More Sheffield Memories - 1 903204 91 7
Memories of Slough - 1 900 463 29 6
Golden Years of Solihull - 1 903204 55 0
Memories of Southampton - 1 900463 34 2
More Memories of Southampton - 1 903204 49 6
Memories of Stockport - 1 900463 55 5
More Memories of Stockport - 1 903204 18 6
Stockport Memories - 1 903204 87 9
Memories of Stockton - 1 900463 41 5
Memories of Stoke-on-Trent - 1 900463 47 4
More Memories of Stoke-on-Trent - 1 903204 12 7
Memories of Stourbridge - 1903204 31 3
Memories of Sunderland - 1 900463 71 7
More Memories of Sunderland - 1 903204 48 8
Sunderland Memories - 1 903 204 95 X
Memories of Swindon - 1 903204 00 3
Memories of Uxbridge - 1 900463 64 4
Memories of Wakefield - 1 900463 65 2
More Memories of Wakefield - 1 900463 89 X
Nostalgic Walsall - 1 900463 18 0
Golden Years of Walsall - 1 903204 56 9
More Memories of Warrington - 1 900463 02 4
Warrington Memories - 1 903204 85 2
Memories of Watford - 1 900463 24 5
Golden Years of West Bromwich - 1 900463 99 7
Memories of Wigan - 1 900463 85 7
Golden Years of Wigan - 1 900463 82 2
More Memories of Wigan - 1 903204 82 8
Nostalgic Wirral - 1 903204 15 1
Wirral Memories - 1 903204 747
Memories of Woking - 1 903204 32 1
Nostalgic Wolverhampton - 1 900463 53 9
Wolverhampton Memories - 1 903204 50 X
Memories of Worcester - 1 903204 25 9
Memories of Wrexham - 1 900463 23 7
Memories of York - 1 900463 66 0
More Memories of York - 1 903 204 94 1